1 MONTH OF
FREE
READING

at
www.ForgottenBooks.com

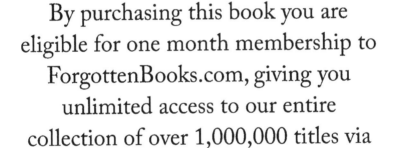

By purchasing this book you are eligible for one month membership to ForgottenBooks.com, giving you unlimited access to our entire collection of over 1,000,000 titles via our web site and mobile apps.

To claim your free month visit:

www.forgottenbooks.com/free265765

ISBN 978-0-428-19501-4
PIBN 10265765

ANNUAL REPORTS

OF

THE TRUSTEES

OF THE

PEABODY ACADEMY OF SCIENCE.

1874 TO 1884

SALEM:

PRINTED FOR THE ACADEMY.

1885.

Mus. 120. 20. 9. 13
Gift of the Academy
Rec. May 1 1805

CONTENTS.

(iii)

NOTE.

The last report published by the Peabody Academy of Science was that of 1873, since which time many changes have been made in the official corps and in the work of the Academy. The present number contains sufficient data, to cover the interval of the ten years up to, and including, 1883. To this have been added the various reports for 1884, with lists of the Trustees and officers and the Academy's publications. Of the earlier reports only a synopsis is given of each; those from 1880 and onward, however, are printed in full. A sketch of the Summer School of Biology, from its inception to its close, with a list of the lecturers and the students, is given separately from the reports, and a paper upon the native woods of Essex County, extracted from Prof. C. S. Sargent's recently published report on the forests of North America, is printed as an appendix. At the annual meeting of the Trustees of the Academy, held February 18, 1885, the reports and accompanying matter were presented and ordered by vote to be printed forthwith.

JOHN ROBINSON,
Editor.

East India Marine Hall,
March 4, 1885.
(iv)

THE ACADEMY:

SOURCES OF ITS COLLECTIONS; THE MUSEUM.

THE Peabody Academy of Science was founded by George Peabody of London in 1867 and incorporated in 1868. The Academy occupies East India Marine Hall, Salem, erected by the East India Marine Society in 1824 and which was purchased and refitted by the trustees of the Academy in 1867.

The collections embrace the museum of the East India Marine Society commenced in 1799 and the Natural History Collection of the Essex Institute commenced in 1834, which were received as permanent deposits, besides accessions since made by the above named societies and the trustees of the Academy.

The museum is open, free to the public, every week day from 9 until 5 o'clock, the average number of visitors for sixteen years having been upwards of 36,000 annually.

The museum contains, on the western side of the hall, a collection illustrating the orders of the animal kingdom, arranged in their proper sequence from the lowest form to the highest.. The most striking features are the Corals, Reptiles, Birds and the Australian Marsupials. This collection was chiefly derived from the Essex Institute in 1867.

On the eastern side is arranged the Ethnological collection, principally received from the East India Marine Society, which is subdivided according to races or countries. This collection ranks in importance among the very highest in America. It is especially rich in idols, models, cloths and domestic utensils from the South Sea Islands,

(1)

implements of war and of domestic use, clothing, ornaments and models of boats from Africa, Arabia, North and South America, Korea, China, Japan and the East Indies as well as life-size models of the natives from the three latter countries.

The gallery cases are devoted to the Zoölogy, Botany and Archæology of Essex County. Nearly every species of its flora and fauna is represented by preserved specimens; the collection of birds and that of native woods are especially full and the collection of prehistoric implements and utensils of stone, bone and pottery from Essex County is a large and excellent one.

Donations to the Academy are solicited, especially in the departments of Ethnology and local Natural History and Archæology. All such will be gratefully acknowledged and properly cared for.

TRUSTEES AND OFFICERS.

The management of the affairs of the Academy is placed in the hands of nine trustees chosen for life, who are empowered to fill vacancies in their board, and officers appointed by them.

Trustees designated by Mr. Peabody, Feb. 26, 1867.

Francis Peabody, of Salem, died Oct. 30, 1867.
Asa Gray, of Cambridge, resigned June 29, 1876.
William Crowninshield Endicott, of Salem.
George Peabody Russell, of England.
Othniel Charles Marsh, of New Haven.
Henry Wheatland, of Salem.
Abner Chaney Goodell, Jr., of Salem.
James Robinson Nichols, of Haverhill.
Henry Coit Perkins, of Newburyport, died Feb. 1, 1873.

Since chosen by the Trustees to fill Vacancies.

Samuel Endicott Peabody, of Salem, Jan. 14, 1868.
George Cogswell, of Bradford, June 25, 1875.
John Robinson, of Salem, June 25, 1875.

OFFICERS OF THE TRUSTEES.

PRESIDENTS.

Francis Peabody, March to October, 1867.
William Crowninshield Endicott, 1868——.

VICE PRESIDENTS.

William Crowninshield Endicott, 1867 to 1868.
Henry Wheatland, 1868——.

SECRETARY.

Abner Chaney Goodell, Jr., 1867——.

TREASURERS.

George Peabody Russell, 1867 to 1870.
Samuel Endicott Peabody, 1870 to 1871.
James Robinson Nichols, 1871 to 1875——.
John Robinson, 1875——.

ACCOUNTANT.

Benjamin Webb Russell, 1867——.

OFFICERS APPOINTED BY THE TRUSTEES.

DIRECTORS OF THE MUSEUM.

Frederick Ward Putnam, 1868 to 1875.
Alpheus Spring Packard, Jr., 1876 to 1878.
Edward Sylvester Morse, 1880——.

CURATORS AND ASSISTANTS.

Alpheus Hyatt, Curator, 1868 to 1870.

Alpheus Spring Packard, Curator, 1868 to 1876.

Edward Sylvester Morse, Curator, 1868 to 1870.

Caleb Cooke, Assistant, 1869 to 1875.   Curator, 1875 to 1880.

Edwin Bicknell, Preparator, 1869 to 1870.

John Sterling Kingsley, Curator, 1877 to 1879.

James Henry Emerton, Curator (in charge of Museum), 1878 to 1880.

John Henry Sears, Assistant, 1880——.

Arthur Robinson Stone, Assistant, 1884.

JANITORS.

William M'Grane, 1867 to 1880.

John Russell Treadwell, 1881——.

NECROLOGY.

GEORGE PEABODY.

Founder of the Peabody Academy of Science February 26, 1867.   Born in Danvers (now Washington Street, Peabody), February 18, 1795.   Died in London, November 4, 1869.

FRANCIS PEABODY.

Son of Joseph and Elizabeth (Smith) Peabody, was born in Salem, December 7, 1801.   As early as 1827 Mr. Peabody was instrumental in establishing courses of scientific lectures in Salem, to which courses he contributed several lectures upon the steam engine, electricity and galvanism; and, at the organization of the Salem Lyceum, he took a leading part.   This was the first movement toward popular scientific lectures now so universal throughout the country·

Mr. Peabody was actively engaged in commercial and manufacturing enterprises throughout his life. In May, 1865, he was chosen President of the Essex Institute, and in 1867 became the first named trustee of the Peabody Academy of Science under Mr. Peabody's letter of trust, and was at once chosen its president. His death occurred October 31, 1867.

HENRY COIT PERKINS.

Son of Thomas and Elizabeth (Storey) Perkins, was born in Newburyport, November 13, 1804. He was graduated at Harvard College 1824 and studied medicine with Dr. Richard S. Spofford of Newburyport and Dr. John C. Warren of Boston. He received the degree of M.D. at Harvard in 1827 and settled in Newburyport. In 1828 he married Harriet, daughter of John Davenport, of Newburyport, by whom he had one son.

Dr. Perkins was one of the trustees of the Academy named by Mr. Peabody in his letter of trust in 1867.

CALEB COOKE.

Son of William and Mary (Fogg) Cooke, was born in Salem, Feb. 5, 1836. He was educated in the public schools of Salem and became a clerk in the book-store of Henry Whipple and Son. He afterward studied with Geo. F. Reed and soon joined the class of students under Prof. Agassiz, at Cambridge. In 1859 he went to Brazil to collect for the Museum of Comparative Zoology, and in 1860 he visited Zanzibar for similar purposes. Upon the foundation of the Academy he at once became associated with its work and in 1875 was made curator of Mollusca. He died in Salem June 5, 1880, after thirteen years of faithful service in the employ of this institution.

PUBLICATIONS.

MEMOIRS (quarto).

No. 1. Revision of the Large Stylated Fossorial Crickets, by Samuel H. Scudder. 33 pages, 1 plate. March, 1869. $1.00.

No. 2. Embryological Studies on Diplax, Perithemis, and the Thysanurous Isotoma, by Alpheus S. Packard, Jr. 24 pages, 3 plates. March, 1871. $1.00.

No. 3. Embryological Studies on Hexapodous Insects, by Alpheus S. Packard, Jr. 18 pages, 3 plates. April, 1872. $1.00.

No. 4. Fresh-water Shell Mounds of the St. John's River, Florida. By Jeffries Wyman. 94 pages, 9 plates. December, 1875. $2.00.

No. 5. Contributions to the Anatomy of the Holothurians, by J. S. Kingsley. 14 pages, 2 plates. May, 1881. 75 cents.

No. 6. On the Development of the Pluteus of Arbacia, by J. Walter Fewkes. 10 pages, 1 plate. May, 1881. 75 cents.

REPORTS (octavo).

FIRST. Work of the Academy, Reports of Curators, Condition of the Museum, 1867–8, Proceedings and letters in connection with the establishment of the institution, agreements with Essex Institute, E. I. M. Society, Description of Cyclocardia Novangliæ, by Edw. S. Morse, etc. 103 pages. Jan., 1869. 75 cents.

SECOND AND THIRD. Work of the Academy, Reports of Curators, Condition of the Museum, 1869–70, Proceedings at Dedication of the Museum, the President's Address, etc., Notes on Rossia palpebrosa, A. Hyatt. Catalogue Batrachia, etc., from Nicaragua, coll. T. A. McNeil, by E. D. Cope.

Catalogue Batrachia, etc., from Florida, coll. C. J. Maynard, by E. D. Cope.

List of Insects from Pebas, Ecuador, by A. S. Packard, Jr.

List of Crustacea from Central America, coll. J. A. McNiel, by Sidney I. Smith. 98 pages, 1871. 75 cents.

FOURTH. Work of the Academy, Reports of Curators, Condition of the Museum, 1871.

Synopsis of the Family Heterofygi, by F. W. Putnam.

A systematic revision of some of the American Butterflies, with notes on Essex County species, by Samuel H. Scudder.

New American Moths, Zygænidæ and Bombycidæ, by A. S. Packard, Jr.

List of Coleoptera collected in Labrador, by A. S. Packard, Jr.

Record of American Entomology for the year 1871, by A. S. Packard, Jr. 147 pages. 1872. 75 cents.

FIFTH.   Work of Academy, Reports of Curators, Condition of the Museum, 1872.

Synopsis of the Thysanura of Essex County, by A. S. Packard, Jr.

Descriptions of New American Phalænidæ, by A. S. Packard, Jr.

Notes on N. A. Phalænidæ and Pyralidæ in the British Museum, by A. S. Packard, Jr.

On the Cave Fauna of Indiana, by A. S. Packard, Jr.

. Record of American Entomology for 1872, by A. S. Packard, Jr. 135 pages. 1873. 75 cents.

SIXTH.   Work of the Academy, Reports of Curators, Condition of the Museum, 1873.

On the Noctuidæ of N. A., by Aug. R. Grote.

Descriptions of New N. A. Phalænidæ, by A. S. Packard, Jr.

New N. A. Phyllopoda, by A. S. Packard, Jr.

Dredgings made near Salem, by A. S. Packard, Jr., and C. Cooke, by A. E. Verrill.

Record of American Entomology for 1873, by A. S. Packard, Jr. 114 pages. 1874. 75 cents.

SEVENTH TO SEVENTEENTH.   Proceedings of the Trustees, work of the Academy, Condition of the Museum from 1874 to 1884.

Account of the Summer School of Biology, Accessions to the Museum and Library.

The Native Woods of Essex County, Mass., their strength, fuel value, etc., as shown by tests upon specimens furnished by the Academy. Extracted from the report on

the Forests of North America, by Prof. C.
S. Sargent; with notice of the report and
tables, prepared by John Robinson. 100
pages, 1885. 75 cents.

SPECIAL PUBLICATIONS.

The American Naturalist, a popular illustrated
magazine of natural history. Edited at first
by A. S. Packard, Jr., E. S. Morse, A.
Hyatt and F. W. Putnam. Vols. 1–11, 1867
to 1877.

This publication is now edited by E. D. Cope
and A. S. Packard, and is published by
McCalla and Stavely of Philadelphia. There
are not many sets remaining and a few numbers are missing in each set. $30.00 per set
(Vols. 1 to 11).

Check-list of the ferns of North America north
of Mexico, by John Robinson, revised by
Prof. D. C. Eaton. Octavo, 13 pages,
printed on one side only, for labelling. July,
1876. 15 cents.

Primitive Industry. Illustrations of the handi-
work, in Stone, Bone and Clay, of the Native Races of the North Atlantic Seaboard
of America, by Charles C. Abbott. Octavo,
460 pages, 429 figures, 1881. $3.00.

NOTE—All communications in relation to the above should be addressed to
John Robinson, Treas., P. A. S., Salem, Mass.

SCHEDULE OF VISITORS TO THE MUSEUM.

Visitors to the Museum, since first opened to the public May 5, 1869.

1869, May to Dec.	26,168.	Closed on Mondays and at noon.
1870, " " "	37,865.	" " " " " "
1871, " " "	51,417.	" " " " " " •
1872, " " "	37,272.	" " " " " "
1873, " " "	39.539.	Closed at noon.
1874, " " "	37,591.	" " "
1875, " " "	36,099.	" " "
1876, " " "	36,509.	" " "
1877, " " "	33,776.	" " "
1878, " " "	34.978.	" " "
1879, " " "	30,625.	" " "
1880, " " "	35,461.	" " "
1881, " " "	37,934.	" " "
1882, " " "	36,676.	" " "
1883, " " "	36.056.	" " "
1884, " " "	38,251.	Open at noon after May 1.
Total, May 1869 to Dec., 1884,	586,217.	
Annual average,	36,638.	

PROCEEDINGS

OF

THE TRUSTEES

1874 - - - 1884.

ABSTRACTS FROM THE RECORDS OF THE

SECRETARY.

PROCEEDINGS OF THE TRUSTEES.

1874, July 4, being a legal holiday, there was no meeting of the Board.

1875, June 12. Annual meeting adjourned from previous dates. Reports read and accepted. Adjourned to June 19 and again to June 26, at which date the officers were chosen for the year. Dr. George Cogswell of Bradford was unanimously chosen trustee to fill the vacancy caused by the death of Dr. Henry C. Perkins of Newburyport. The resignation of S. Endicott Peabody was read and accepted and John Robinson of Salem was unanimously chosen a trustee to fill the vacancy.

1875, June 29. Dr. Asa Gray retired as trustee having previously sent in his resignation.

1875, September 10. The resignations of F. W. Putnam as Director of the Museum and that of A. S. Packard, Jr., as curator, were accepted. Caleb Cooke was appointed Curator of Mollusca. The affairs of the museum were placed in the hands of the council during the vacancy in the office of director. Dr. Nichols resigned his office as Treasurer and John Robinson was chosen to fill the place. S. Endicott Peabody was unanimously chosen to fill the vacancy caused by the resignation of Dr. Gray.

1876, March 3. The adjourned annual meeting. The officers were chosen for the year. The annual appropriations for the museum were voted and the matters pertaining to the museum were placed in the hands of the Executive Committee. The establishment of a Summer School of Biology was referred to the Executive Committee with

(13)

power to act, and the Director and Treasurer authorized to employ certain funds to build a suitable building for a laboratory. A. S. Packard, Jr., was chosen Director.

1877, Feb. 9. Adjourned annual meeting. Officers were chosen for the year. It was voted to establish the Summer School on the basis upon which it was conducted the past season. John S. Kingsley was appointed Curator of Palæontology, Mineralogy and Crustacea.

1878, Jan. 18. Adjourned annual meeting. Officers were chosen for the year. The Summer School, report of Director and other matters were referred to the Executive Committee.

1878, August 3. A. S. Packard, Jr., tendered his resignation as Director to take effect Sept. 1, which was accepted. The President was requested to tender to Dr. Packard the thanks of the Trustees for his valuable services and express to him their sincere wishes for his future success. John Robinson was chosen Director *pro tem.*, with full power of Director after Sept. 1, and authorized to secure the services of Jas. H. Emerton for museum work.

1879, Feb. 7. Adjourned annual meeting. Officers chosen for the year. Jas. H. Emerton was appointed Curator in charge of the Museum.

1879, July 19. The matter of issuing licenses to shoot birds and collect eggs under the statute of 1877 was referred to the Treasurer and Curator with full powers.

1880, Feb. 20. Adjourned annual meeting. Officers were chosen for the year. Appropriations were voted to be expended under the authority of the Executive Committee.

1880, July 3. The death of Caleb Cooke, which occurred June 5, was announced, and the President was requested to communicate the sympathy of the Trustees to the mother of Mr. Cooke and express to her their appreciation of his faithful services to the Academy. The Executive Committee reported that they had accepted the resignation of Mr. J. H. Emerton as Curator in charge of the Museum and that Mr. E. S. Morse had been appointed to fill the vacancy. This action was approved. Edward S. Morse was chosen Director of the Museum. Mr. Morse came before the Board and gave an outline of proposed future work for the Academy recommending the development of the Ethnological collection, the perfecting of the collections of the Flora and Fauna of Essex County, the arrangement of a typical Zoölogical collection, and made suggestions in relation to the library. John H. Sears was appointed assistant at the Museum.

1881, Feb. 25. Adjourned annual meeting. The officers were chosen, the reports read and accepted and the appropriations for the year passed to be expended by authority of the Executive Committee. Various matters suggested in the report of the Director were referred to the Executive Committee.

1883, Feb. 16. Adjourned annual meeting. The officers were chosen for the year and the reports read and accepted.

1883, Dec. 4. The Director having been absent on leave by authority of the Executive Committee, and Mr. Robinson having been placed in charge of the Museum during his absence, it was voted, in order that Mr. Morse may be more at liberty to perform certain literary work, that the President make such arrangements between the Treasurer and Director for this purpose as may be mutually satisfactory until the next annual meeting, at which time he was to report a plan for the future arrangement of their work. A committee, consisting of Messrs. Peabody, Cogswell and Robinson, was appointed to consider the expediency of building an addition to East India Marine Hall and to report at the annual meeting.

1884, Feb. 22. Adjourned annual meeting. The reports of the Director and Treasurer were read and accepted.

It was voted that a condensed report of the proceedings of the Trustees of the Academy since the last printed report together with the reports of the officers of the Academy be printed under the direction of the Executive Committee. The officers for the year were chosen.

The President, in accordance with a vote at a previous meeting, presented a report of a plan of arrangement of the duties of Director and Treasurer to the effect:

1. That Mr. Morse continue as Director for the years 1884 and 1885.

2. That when in Salem he shall visit the museum four mornings each week for consultation, advising and directing in regard to the work in progress or in regard to any change or enlargement of the museum.

3. That he shall make his annual report as usual and consult with the Trustees whenever they shall desire his presence.

4. That he shall deliver six lectures, annually, upon subjects of Natural History under direction of the Trustees.

5. That otherwise he shall devote his time to his proposed books on Japan and deliver lectures on his own account.

6. That he shall retain the title of Director of the Peabody Academy of Science in any books he may publish, and in any lectures, papers or other documents he may deliver or sign he shall be described by that title.

7. That arrangements shall be made to procure, if ossible, copies of Mr. Morse's bo oks on the Japanese for the exchanges of the Academy.

8. That Mr. Robinson shall continue as Trustee, and,

in the absence of Mr. Morse, hold the place and perform the duties of acting Director.

9. That he shall have full charge of all assistants and persons employed in the Academy, arrange the hours of work and for the opening and closing of the hall; have control, with advice of the Director, of all objects in the collections and in the Museum and generally perform all the duties of Director not attended to by Mr. Morse.

It was voted that the recommendations in the report be adopted. The President then read the report of the committee to whom was referred the extension of East India Marine Hall for the enlargement of the Museum.

The report recommended that an addition, fifty by sixty feet and two stories in height, be built to correspond with the present structure on the eastern side of the Academy's land as appeared by a plan presented. The cost of this addition ready for cases would be about $15,000. The expenditure and work might be extended over a period of three years. The committee also recommended that the Trustees authorize them to proceed at once to erect such an addition as was suggested. It was voted that the report be accepted and the recommendations be adopted, and that the sum of $2,000 be appropriated to begin the work, the committee consisting of the President, Treasurer, Dr. Cogswell and Mr. Peabody.

1884, July 5. It was voted that the building of an extension to East India Marine Hall be deferred until the spring of 1885, and, in the meantime, that the committee having this matter in charge be requested to have plans, specifications and estimates made to be presented at the annual meeting for consideration and, if then it should be deemed advisable, operations be commenced as soon as the state of the weather permitted.

ANNUAL REPORTS

OF THE

OFFICERS IN CHARGE

OF THE

MUSEUM.

1874---1883.

ANNUAL REPORTS.

. 1874.

SEVENTH ANNUAL REPORT.

ABSTRACT OF REPORT OF F. W. PUTNAM, DIRECTOR OF THE MUSEUM.

THE work of the Academy for the year was mainly in the line of that of the previous year. The Director continued his researches upon the fishes and upon archæological matters. Doctor Packard devoted his time to the articulata upon which branch he was continually employed. Mr. Cooke made several changes in the arrangement of the specimens in the museum and continued his attention to the alcoholic collections. The Director having been placed in temporary charge of the archæological cabinet of the Peabody Museum of Archæology to fill the vacancy caused by the death of Prof. Jeffries Wyman, he was obliged to spend a portion of the time each week in Cambridge.

The number of visitors for the year was 37,501. The accessions to the library were of a similar character to those of previous years.

To the museum several important additions were made. Dr. Chas. C. Abbott of Trenton continued to add to his valuable collection of prehistoric relics from New Jersey presented previously and an interesting collection of objects was received through the Essex Institute, the result of an exploration of "Indian graves" at Marblehead. One perfect skeleton was preserved (a re-burial), together with several implements and an earthen pot. There was also received a very valuable collection of Australian mammals and birds from Mr. Chas. Foster. This collec-

(21)

tion also included a large number of marsupials entirely new to the museum which, together with the mammals, were sent to the establishment of Mr. Ward of Rochester, N. Y., for preparation. The birds were mounted by Mr. Welch and Mr. Vickary. Mr. S. E. Cassino remained as a student with Dr. Packard and continued to work upon the collections.

1875.

EIGHTH ANNUAL REPORT.

ABSTRACT OF REPORT OF A. S. PACKARD, JR., IN CHARGE OF MUSEUM.

THE museum work consisted chiefly in the re-arrangement of the insects, corals, crustacea and worms to which groups many specimens were added. Mr. Cooke also began an arrangement of the mollusca. The skeleton of a blackfish captured on Beverly bar in 1873, and since in the hands of Mr. H. A. Ward for preparation, was placed in the museum as also were the Australian marsupials, mammals and birds presented by Mr. C. H. Foster.

Mr. Robinson began the arrangement of the Essex County herbarium to which some 150 species of native plants were added. In October, a living spike of flowers of the Century Plant from the garden of H. H. Hunnewell, Esq., of Wellesley, was placed on exhibition in the hall.

A case was prepared for the reception of recent accessions to the museum and lists of such were published in the Salem papers. 36,099 persons visited the museum during the year, and 92 donations were received from 73 persons.

A class from the Salem High School attended three courses of lectures under the auspices of the Academy, given as follows: Mr. Putnam, five lectures on Fishes; Doctor Packard, five lectures on Insects and Crustacea; Mr. Robinson, five lectures on Botany. There were two special students at the Academy, Mr. S. E. Cassino of Salem, taking up branches of entomology and Mr. J. S. Kingsley of Norwich, N. Y., studying the crustacea. Mr. Putnam resigned as director in October to accept the position of permanent curator of the Peabody Museum of Archæology at Cambridge.

1876.

NINTH ANNUAL REPORT.

ABSTRACT OF REPORT OF A. S. PACKARD, JR., DIRECTOR.

THE principal work on the collections in the museum was the re-arrangement of the shells by Mr. Cooke and of the crustacea and worms by Mr. Kingsley. Mr. Robinson continued his work on the Essex County plants adding 456 species to the herbarium, and Mr. John H. Sears presented 30 species of native woods. Dr. Packard's time was devoted to the insects, chiefly upon the geometrid moths. A full set (25 vols.) of the Proceedings of the American Association for the Advancement of Science were added to the library and, to the museum, the most important gift was the collection of objects from China, including models, tools, *materia medica*, etc., received through the Essex Institute from Mr. J. L. Hammond of Salem, commissioner in the Chinese department of the Centennial Exhibition at Philadelphia. Donations were received during the year from 80 individuals, and 36,509 persons visited the museum.

A collection including 100 species of beetles, birds, mammals, etc., were deposited in the cabinet of the Manning High School at Ipswich. Mr. Arthur F. Gray and Mr. S. E. Cassino were for limited times students at the Academy, and Mr. J. S. Kingsley continued his studies through the year on the crustacea and also assisted in museum work.

Mr. Robinson delivered four lectures on Botany in various parts of the county. A summer school of biology was opened in July attended by seventeen students. The fourth memoir, "The Fresh Water Shell Mounds of the St. John's River of Florida," by the late Dr. Jeffries Wyman, was issued during the year.

1877.

TENTH ANNUAL REPORT.

ABSTRACT OF THE REPORT OF A. S. PACKARD, JR., DIRECTOR.

The work of the Academy for this year, in addition to conducting the summer school, consisted chiefly in the rearrangement of the crustacea and minerals by Mr. J. S. Kingsley, the continued work on the shells by Mr. Cooke and the completion of the Essex County collection of woods by Mr. Robinson and Mr. Sears.

The Director devoted much time to the geometrid moths and through his efforts valuable additions were made to the collections from V. T. Chambers of Covington, Ky., and Messrs. Edwards and Behrens of San Francisco, Cal. Mr. Edward M. Shepard of Norfolk, Conn., came to the Academy as a special student in February, remaining several months. He devoted his time to the study of articulata and plants.

Prof. R. Ramsay Wright during the summer months was at the Academy for the purpose of studying the sponges; during which time he gratuitously gave a course of lectures on the vertebrates to the students at the summer school.

The working force of the U. S. Fish Commission, under direction of Prof. S. F. Baird, had its headquarters at Salem during the summer. The Academy received many kind attentions from the gentlemen connected with the commission, especially from Messrs. Goode and Bean, who named some fifty species of fishes in the cabinet of the Museum.

The session of the summer school for the year was very successful, being attended by twenty-one students. The condition of the museum was much improved during the year by cleaning the cases and re-arranging many groups of specimens. 104 donations were received from 61 individuals and 33,776 persons visited the hall. In November a number of persons, interested in the study of botany, formed a class called the Botanical Section of the Peabody Academy of Science and meetings were held for mutual improvement in botanical study. Dr. G. A. Perkins was chosen Chairman, Miss Lucy H. Upton, Secretary, and John Robinson, Treasurer. About twenty-five persons joined the Section.

1878.

ELEVENTH ANNUAL REPORT.

ABSTRACT OF REPORT OF JOHN ROBINSON, DIRECTOR, PRO TEM.

The most notable event during the year was the resignation of Dr. A. S. Packard, Jr., as Director, which took effect September first, he having accepted the chair of Geology at Brown University, Providence, R. I. Mr. James H. Emerton was appointed Curator in charge of the museum September first. Mr. Emerton devoted his entire time to the care of the museum and the increase of the Essex County zoölogical collections, adding some 200 specimens at once to the number of county invertebrates, the result of his work during the summer at the seashore. Sixteen students attended the session of the summer school and twenty-five persons attended the meetings of the Botanical Section.

A large amount of work was done on the collections. Mr. Kingsley arranged and catalogued the crustacea, Mr. Cooke continued the arrangement of the mollusca and Mr. Robinson the work on the herbarium by re-arranging the North American and foreign plants. 123 accessions were received from 100 individuals and institutions and 34,978 persons visited the museum during the year. Mr. Emerton devoted one hour each day through the fall months to the explanation of the specimens in the zoölogical collection to such visitors as were present and began the preparation of a guide to the museum.

1879.

TWELFTH ANNUAL REPORT.

ABSTRACT OF REPORT OF J. H. EMERTON, CURATOR, IN CHARGE OF MUSEUM.

The work for the year was chiefly upon the zoölogical specimens in the museum. Rubber strips were placed upon all the cases, the specimens thoroughly fumigated and the alcoholic specimens properly cared for. The dried plants were all placed in a case in one of the lower rooms to be more accessible for study and the work on the Essex County collection was continued. A very large number of plants, including a set of North American ferns, a set of Austin's Hepaticæ and other specimens desirable for reference, were added from Mr. Robinson's herbarium. The summer school was attended by five students; the lectures were all given by Mr. Emerton who, in the spring, gave a course of lectures to teachers and others on the animals of Essex County. In the fall Mr. Emerton repeated the lectures given by him at the summer school to a class of young persons from Salem. From February to May and again from October to December, arrangements were made to have daily skimmings taken of the surface water at the Essex bridge. These skimmings, teeming with animal life, were examined at the Academy and all desirable specimens thus collected were either preserved in alcohol or mounted on microscope slides. In July and August, Mr. Emerton conducted dredgings in the harbor and the animals thus obtained were named by Profs. Verrill and Smith of New Haven. A guide to the museum was published during the year, of which a large number of copies were sold and distributed. The meetings of the Botanical Section were successfully continued in the same manner as during the two previous years. 30,625 persons visited the museum and during the year, 61 donations were received to the cabinet from fifty different persons.

1880.

THIRTEENTH ANNUAL REPORT.

REPORT OF EDWARD S. MORSE, DIRECTOR.

I HAVE the honor to submit the following report of the Academy's operations since my appointment in July.

At your semi-annual meeting in July a plan of work, but partially matured at the time, was presented by me. In this plan it was urged that the Academy should relinquish all efforts towards building up a large general collection, as it could not hope to compete with the great museums of the Boston Society of Natural History and the

Museum of Comparative Zoölogy at Cambridge. Any attempt to rival these institutions, with their large endowments and corps of trained assistants, would not only be impossible, but with such ready access to them, undesirable. The Academy should, however, endeavor to perfect those departments which already give it preëminence above all other museums in the country.

The museum of the Academy is already widely known by its unrivalled ethnological collections, the result of the intelligent interest of Salem sea captains, who, during the height of Salem's commerce, founded the East India Marine Society, and the collections of animals and plants of Essex County, the results of the slow and painstaking efforts of a few devoted students, who founded the Essex County Natural History Society, afterwards merged in the Essex Institute.

While a great number of valuable additions have since been made to the collections, the museum, as it stands to-day, is strongest in the two collections above named; the one embracing objects pertaining to man, gathered from all parts of the world; the other embracing the animals and plants of Essex County.

The Academy, by concentrating its efforts to enlarge these collections and perfect their arrangement, has within its power the ability to make a museum that shall stand among the first of its kind and be an honor to its liberal founder.

With this object in view, every effort should be made towards completely arranging and labelling the collections already in its possession. Thus far it has been impossible to make much headway in this work, for lack of room. For a long time the exhibition cases have been over crowded. The long upright cases, now nearly completed, will give the desired room for a re-arrangement of the zoölogical collections, which are to be arranged on one side of the hall; leaving the other side for the display of the ethnological collections. A partition has been made in the central cases, thus more perfectly dividing the hall for this purpose; and giving much better light for the display of the specimens.

It is proposed to arrange the ethnological collections according to the countries from which they come, and not according to the generic character of the objects. At present the musical instruments are gathered together in one case, the weapons in another and so on. It is now proposed to re-arrange the collection by countries, so that a student may get at a glance an idea of the culture of any people. By this arrangement, also, the deficiencies in the collection may be more readily seen. Systematic efforts will then be made to strengthen those portions of the collection which are particularly weak, either by exchange or direct purchase. The Academy's large stock of duplicates may here be used advantageously.

The Academy has continued to receive the publications of American and foreign societies, for which no adequate return has yet been made. At the semi-annual meeting in July, the trustees decided to resume the publication of the memoirs, and with this decision the director issued a circular letter to its home and foreign correspondents thanking contributors for their continued favors and stating that a return might soon be expected.

The necessity of a scientific library connected with the Academy has always been recognized by the trustees. The purchase of books involves great expense. The securing of books by an exchange of its own publications, while involving less expense, accomplishes a far more important object in bringing the Academy into the ranks of similar institutions at home and abroad by contributing to the world the results of original researches. In this light the Academy is justified in making a small annual appropriation for the purpose of resuming and continuing its memoirs.

Since July 1, 1880, the Academy has received in volumes and parts of volumes, reports and catalogues, a total of three hundred and sixty-one numbers. These mostly embrace the transactions of foreign societies.

The liberal appropriation for the fifth session of the summer school of biology was expended in securing the assistance of instructors eminent in their respective departments. The Academy had the rare good fortune of securing the services of Prof. Geo. L. Goodale, of Harvard University, for a limited course of lectures on Physiological Botany, as well as the services of Mr. H. H. Straight of the Oswego Normal School, Mr. J. Walter Fewkes of the Museum of Comparative Zoölogy and Mr. Chas. Fish of Orono, Maine, as instructors, respectively, on the anatomy and physiology of the vertebrates, cœlenterates and insects. Mr. John Robinson kindly volunteered his services in a course of lectures on cryptogamic botany and Mr. John H. Sears gave special instruction in structural and analytical botany.

The director wishes to record the valuable services rendered gratuitously by Dr. Geo. M. Sternberg of the United States Army. As a skilful microscopist he aided the class in preparing objects, directing them in microscopical manipulation, and gave two special lectures on Bacteria and how to use the microscope.

Besides the laboratory instruction, forty-seven stated lectures were given by the gentlemen above named.

It was a matter of surprise that but three of the students came from Essex County, as special efforts were made to secure them from this region. Owing to the strain upon instructors and students alike, the summer schools have been looked upon by many professional men as seriously interfering with that recreation and rest which those who engage in the work particularly need. Both instructors and students are, with few exceptions, teachers. The class fatigued with their own duties as teachers throughout the year come before tired instructors. In our own case two of the pupils broke down within a week after the school commenced. In consultation with Mr. Agassiz, Dr. Goodale and others I find similar experiences have occurred elsewhere. A seaside laboratory like that of Mr. Agassiz's at Newport, or Dr. Anton Dohrn's at Naples, to which students resort for the purpose of pursuing special investigation, is quite different from a summer school, where a tired pupil is dragged over the realms of the animal and plant kingdom, in the limited space of six weeks. While it is not desirable to abandon the summer school, some judicious modifications in regard to the length of the term and work may partially remedy the objections above alluded to.

Heretofore the term has been one of six weeks' duration. In this time has been crowded all the instruction in Botany and Zoölogy. It is now suggested that the term shall not exceed four weeks in length, and that two separate and distinct classes shall be formed : one relating especially to Zoölogy and the other to Botany. The pupils of each class being allowed to attend, in common, all the stated lectures. With this plan the same amount of work will be accomplished, while those engaged in the work will have two additional weeks of recreation. The cost of tuition to the pupil as well as the expense incurred for instruction will be lessened in proportion.

It is furthermore proposed, with the approval of the trustees, that instructors shall be secured, who can give a few additional hours each day to labelling and otherwise arranging the collections of the Academy, which come within their respective provinces. By such a plan, the Academy will be able to have the arrangement of its special collections gradually perfected under the guidance of experts in each department.

The Academy has to deplore the loss of Mr. Caleb Cooke, who has been connected with the institution since its foundation. Formerly a student at the Museum of Comparative Zoölogy, under Agassiz, he assisted in the arrangement of the collections in the new Museum. He had continued in work of a similar nature up to the time of his death. While connected with the Cambridge Museum he was sent to Para, South America, and to Zanzibar, Africa, on collecting tours. During his connection with the Academy he had become familiar with all its departments, and done much work in arranging the collections of shell and other animals.

In his death the Academy lost a faithful and conscientious assistant, whose loss will be seriously felt in the active work of the museum.

Mr. John H. Sears, of Danvers, who has for several years been more or less familiar with the work and objects of the Academy, was appointed to fill his place. Mr. Sears has made a special study of Botany, both practical and scientific. As a teacher in analytical botany he has conducted classes with success, and the Academy is fortunate in being able to command his services.

The Director has, during the year, devised a plan for the purpose of utilizing the sun's rays in heating rooms and has made a practical test of the apparatus in the exhibition hall, the air of which in winter is not only very cold but has that dead and chilling effect of a cellar.

As is well known, a black surface absorbs the heat rays of the sun ; an area of thirty-two square feet will absorb theoretically an amount equal to one horse power.

The arrangement already designed and made consists of a box thirteen feet long and four feet wide. This has a front of glass facing the sun. The glass, in narrow strips, is set at an angle, so that its greatest surface is at nearly right angles to the direct rays of the sun in winter. Directly behind the glass is a continuous surface of corrugated sheet iron, painted black. The iron is arranged in such a way that the greatest possible surface is presented to the sun's rays. Behind this iron sheet is an air space of the dimensions of the box, and four inches wide. The lower end of this space communicates directly with the outer air while the upper end opens into the hall. This latter opening is furnished with a lid, so that it can be closed at night and when the sun is obscured by clouds. The back of the box is lined with felting and paper to answer as a non-conductor. The air in this space becoming heated by the sun on the blackened iron, rises and enters the hall to make room for other air which enters the lower end of the box, to be heated in turn, and thus a current of air is caused to pass into the hall, more or less heated by the sun's rays.

A number of experiments were made to show the variations in the temperature of the air at the lower and outer mouth of the heater, and the temperature of the air as it enters the hall. By simple methods it was ascertained that the air passed through the box in from five to seven seconds. On days of great clearness and consequently of high temperature in the box the air passed through the box in the space of five seconds. As the cubic contents of the air space are seventeen cubic feet, the discharge into the hall is equal to twelve thousand, two hundred and

34

forty cubic feet per hour. As the apparatus is fully active for two hours in mid-day and is partially active equal to two hours more, the amount of air discharged into the hall is equal to forty-eight thousand, five hundred and sixty feet during every clear day of sunshine. As the cubic contents of the hall, accounting for the displacement of the cases, is equal to sixty thousand cubic feet, roughly estimated, the air must be entirely replaced every day and a half.

The experiments thus far made are so successful that a larger heater is to be made for further testing the application of this principle.

East India Marine Hall,
Feb. 1, 1881. EDWARD S. MORSE.

1881.

FOURTEENTH ANNUAL REPORT.

REPORT OF EDWARD S. MORSE, DIRECTOR.

I have the honor to submit the following report of work accomplished during the year ending Dec. 31, 1881.

The experience of the year has given no cause to deviate from the plan of operations presented in the last report. This plan urged that special efforts should be made to develop the ethnological and special local collections, and to fully arrange these collections before any extended effort should be made to secure additional contributions.

The new upright cases, made from the plans submitted to the trustees and approved by them, were completed in the early part of the year and in these cases have been permanently mounted and arranged the collections of sponges, corals and sea fans. The cases have fully answered the

object specially aimed at; namely, the display of specimens in an upright position. The cases have received the
approval of others engaged in the work of museum arrangement. The new Museum of the State Agricultural
College of Michigan, just completed, has adopted the
cases without modification. The broad upright tablets
for the display of specimens have worked so well in the
new cases that the plan has been adopted for the remaining cases and with slight modifications the old shelves
have been changed to this form. The plan submitted for
the arrangement of the ethnological collections, after that
followed by the Museum of Ethnology, at Leipsic, has
been commenced.

The material representing China has been permanently
arranged in one of the central cases. A rough grouping
of the other countries has been made, and the permanent
mounting of the Malay group has progressed as far as the
mounting of the weapons. These have been cleaned of
layers of varnish and dirt which had accumulated upon
them at intervals, since they have been in the Museum,
and their appearance has been entirely altered.

It has been impossible to arrange for display, even temporarily, the materials of which the rough grouping has
been made, as the shelves of these cases have been altered
to upright tablets and it was not thought expedient to go
to the expense of temporary shelving. For this reason,
the collection, not permanently arranged, presents anything but an attractive appearance. 370 accessions have
been received from 32 donors, including a large collection of American woods from the Arnold Arboretum,
through Prof. C. S. Sargent. Among the donations
may be specially mentioned a valuable collection of stone
implements from Alfred Osgood, Esq., and a series of

casts of the extinct bird Hesperornis, from Prof. O. C. Marsh.

The visitors to the museum numbered 37,934. The number of visitors for the preceding year being 35,461.

The Director urgently suggests that some other means for warming the work rooms of the Academy, as well as the shops in the front, than those now employed be considered. At present there are five sources of danger in the coal fires used in heating. If some method of steam heating could be provided in which the generators should be outside the building, a great source of danger might be removed. He would also beg leave to call attention to the possible source of danger in the presence of a drug store in the building, and to the fact that fire insurance companies recognize drug stores as hazardous, and he would urge the necessity of securing some tenant whose occupation would entail less risks from fire.

The immense value of the ethnological collections is but faintly appreciated. It is only necessary to state that in many cases the races who used the various objects which adorn the museum, are now extinct; and that books of travel written thirty years ago, describing certain of the objects, record the fact that the natives had for a long time abandoned the manufacture of them, their use being supplanted by the gun and iron knife. If the collection is ever destroyed by fire, it is safe to say, that many of the objects can never be replaced.

LIBRARY.

The additions to the library have increased over those of the preceding year. The volumes and pamphlets received give a total of 466 numbers, representing as donors 84 societies and institutions.

MEMOIRS.

In accordance with the decision of the trustees that the publication of memoirs should be resumed, the director accepted two memoirs, one from Mr. J. S. Kingsley entitled "Contributions to the Anatomy of the Holothurians," illustrated by two folded lithographic plates and containing fourteen pages of printed matter; and the other by Mr. J. Walter Fewkes entitled "The Development of the Pluteus of Abacia," containing ten pages of printed matter and illustrated by one lithographic plate. These were published and immediately forwarded to the Societies with which the Academy is in correspondence. The sum of $500.00 was appropriated for the purpose, but the amount expended for the two memoirs was $202.00. The paper upon which they were printed was already owned by the Academy, there being now on hand enough for the memoirs for several years to come.

SUMMER SCHOOL.

The following instructors were engaged for the sixth session : Physiological Botany, a course of lectures by Prof. D. P. Penhallow; Analytical Botany, instruction by John H. Sears ; Anatomy and Physiology of Vertebrates, lectures and laboratory work by Prof. H. H. Straight, Oswego Normal School ; Embryology, a course of eight lectures by Dr. Chas. S. Minot ; Cœlenterates, a course of six lectures by J. W. Fewkes of the Museum of Comparative Zoölogy ; Entomology, lectures and instruction by Chas. Fish ; Invertebrates, lectures and instruction by Edward S. Morse ; fifty-two lectures and laboratory demonstrations were given.

The attendance was small, the laboratory pupils numbering five and those attending the lectures numbering five. The income from this source amounted to

$65.00, and the total amount expended for instruction and incidental expenses connected with the school amounting to $430.31, leaving a balance of $69.69 unexpended.

The disappointment felt at this result is tempered by the fact that other schools of a similar nature have had a similarly small attendance.

The director is still in doubt as to the best plan to be pursued in the expenditure of the liberal grant made by the trustees for the summer school. It seems wise, however, to continue the instruction in some way, provided some efficient means be devised by which the inhabitants of Essex County shall be more fully benefited by the endowment. He has at present no suggestion to make concerning the matter other than that the annual appropriation may be reduced to $400.00, since with that sum of the money the income from pupils is sure to make up what little deficiencies may arise.

The incidental expenses of the museum have been kept far within the appropriations for the year and a considerable sum realized from various sources, which has been transferred to the treasury. The director would suggest that a limited sum be placed at his disposal for the purpose of purchasing ethnological specimens to fill gaps in the collections, as when opportunities offer for such purchases it is difficult to obtain the proper authority at once.

EDWARD S. MORSE,
East India Marine Hall, *Director.*
Feb. 1, 1882.

1882.

FIFTEENTH ANNUAL REPORT.

REPORT OF JOHN ROBINSON, TREAS., IN CHARGE OF MUSEUM.

In consequence of the sudden departure of the Director for Japan in April last the charge of the Museum came to me as a surprise. The lecturers for the summer school had been engaged and, in the cabinet, the ethnological specimens were in confusion incidental to the entire rearrangement of that department which had been begun the year previous. Being familiar with Mr. Morse's plan, it was my first duty to arrange these specimens so that they should be available to the numerous visitors always present during the summer and fall. This was accomplished quite satisfactorily and, at the same time, labels were placed on a great number of specimens not previously marked.

The system of placing large signs denoting the country to which the specimens belonged was continued and before July the whole collection was placed in very good order.

Many minor changes have been made to improve the appearance of the hall and entry-ways, and large tablets have been placed at the outside door and at the landing on the stairway which briefly state the origin and ownership of the collections.

VISITORS TO THE MUSEUM.

The visitors for the year numbered 36,676. The number on single days being: Fast Day, April 6, 667; July 4, 520; July 20 (Barnum's circus at Salem), 635.

It is important to notice that while the largest number of visitors on any single day is not one-third of the number often noted in previous years, at the same time the total number for the year exceeds that of late years. This is accounted for by the fact that persons who formerly made the museum a rendezvous on public days now go to the "Willows" for that purpose, while those who visit the museum for instruction increase yearly. The

accession of summer residents in Essex County has no-
ticeably affected the number of visitors during July, August and September. It would seem that nearly every
seashore guest between Boston and Portsmouth regarded a
visit to our museum one of their summer duties and
it has been gratifying to hear, nearly every day, com-
ments on the excellent system of arrangement, the labelling of the specimens and the neatness of the building.
Among the visitors during the year was President Arthur,
he being the third president of the United States who
has visited the hall. The Natural History Clubs from
West Newbury and Boxford have each spent a day in the
Museum and efforts were made to encourage them to continue the study of our local fauna and flora.

NEW CASES.

Additional upright cases have been built, corresponding
to those now containing the corals, at a cost considerably
below the former price, besides having them provided
with locks of a very much improved pattern. Storage
cases, containing nearly 200 trays, have also been built in
the lecture-room and attic. In these cases the collection
of shells has been placed.

SUMMER SCHOOL.

The lecturers for the summer school having been engaged during the winter, it was thought best to continue
the issue of the circulars, although Mr. Morse's name was
withdrawn. After an unusual effort had been made, however, but three students, none of whom were from Essex
County, had been secured by July 1st. Therefore, after

consultation with the acting president and the lecturers, it was thought best to give up the regular session of the school. This was more willingly done as Prof. Bessey and Mr. Fewkes agreed to give courses of lectures in Salem during the winter which should be free to teachers and others. These lectures are now in process of delivery, the tickets to the number of 250 having been quickly taken up by the very class of people which we should most desire to reach. The discontinuance of the summer school is the fate of nearly every such institution in the country, ours having survived far longer than most of the others.

BOTANICAL CLASSES.

As the attendance at the summer school has declined that at the sessions of the winter class in botany has yearly increased. This winter two classes were formed, one of twenty members instructed by Mr. Sears in elementary botany, the other, called a botanical section, composed of the older members of the previous classes, numbering nearly twenty-three persons, who study more advanced subjects, under the instruction of the present writer. The meetings of this class have averaged for four years over fifteen regular attendants who have met weekly each winter: the expense of all the classes has not been $100 for the four years. The success of these classes suggests the feasibility of seeking to establish other classes of a similar nature, a plan quite successfully carried out one season by Mr. Emerton, when a class of fifteen was formed to study the animals of Essex County. I would respectfully suggest that a sum be appropriated sufficient to engage a competent teacher of mineralogy and that a class be formed to study the rocks of this region. $150 would probably be enough for this purpose, in addition to a small tuition fee.

ESSEX COUNTY COLLECTIONS.

As soon as a general arrangement of the museum was effected the time was devoted to the Archæology of the county. For years this department had received little or no attention, the specimens having never been separated from those of the general collection. The rapidly increasing interest in this subject has made it difficult to obtain additional specimens and therefore it seemed advisable to purchase, at once, some local collections in Essex County which were on sale. The specimens have now been permanently arranged in the eastern gallery cases and form the best local collection of prehistoric implements in Essex County. The effect of this exhibition has been to secure a large number of gifts from various parts of the county, many of which included valuable specimens.

In October, Mr. I. J. Potter, of Ipswich, called the attention of the Academy to a newly discovered shellheap on Perkins Island, in Ipswich river. This was opened by the Academy and proved to be one of the most interesting yet examined. Every specimen of value was saved and is now placed in the museum. It is the only single shellheap contents we have, as yet, systematically preserved from this county; all previous explorations having been of a desultory character.

ACCESSIONS.

There has been a marked increase in the number of accessions over recent years; upwards of 200 separate donations, including 2,000 specimens of all sorts, have been received from 127 individuals and institutions. It has been the effort of those in charge to acknowledge even the smallest gift, as, oftentimes, the encouragement thus given has been the means of bringing to the museum, from the same persons, specimens of considerable value and importance. Among the more important accessions for the year, besides those otherwise mentioned, are many birds and mammals from Essex County new to the cabinet; South Sea Island cloths, from Miss Mary Derby; a collection illustrating the products of petroleum from Mr. Chas. Toppan of Salem; Implements and Utensils from Africa from Capt. F. King and Mrs. Chas. Hoffman; a cabinet of minerals collected and arranged by the late Samuel Johnson, received through the Essex Institute; a large specimen of quartz crystal from Madagascar, from Capt. W. Beadle of Peabody, and a collection of forty figures illustrating the costumes and trades of Mexico, purchased through Mr. F. Ober, of Beverly.

WOOD-CUTS.

The large collection of wood-cuts of the figures in the American Naturalist and the Memoirs of the Academy, have been arranged in drawers with an impression of each placed on the outside of the block, and a duplicate impression mounted in a blank-book for reference, thus rendering them easy to find and enabling any one to see at once such cuts as are in possession of the Academy.

CALEB COOKE MEMORIAL.

Early in the year, some friends of the late Caleb Cooke, desiring to commemorate his work in our scientific institutions, requested permission to place a memorial tablet in the entrance of the museum. To this proposition the trustees signified their cordial approval and before the close of the year a beautiful mural tablet of terra cotta, especially designed and executed by the Boston Terra Cotta Company, with an appropriate ornamentation and inscription, was placed in position. The tablet was paid for by voluntary contributions, aside from the setting, which was contributed by the Academy's mason, Mr. Peterson. [The tablet was formally presented by the subscribers to the trustees of the Academy on the evening of Jan. 12, 1883.]

LIBRARY AND PUBLICATIONS.

The additions to the library include eleven bound volumes and 355 parts of volumes, pamphlets and serials received from ninety-five institutions and individuals. Upwards of thirty large volumes, chiefly publications of the Smithsonian Institution, which were in frequent use, have been bound and several text and reference books, including a large atlas and a gazetteer, much needed in every day work, have been purchased.

On account of the continued absence of the President and Director, it was thought best to defer the proposed printing of the annual reports and hence no publications have been issued this year, excepting articles concerning the museum in some of our county papers. It would, therefore, seem desirable to issue immediately some publication in return for the exchanges thus far received.

The library increases in size every year and requires both additional care and room. The duplication of books referred to by the Director in his last report still continues, while very few of the books are ever used. I cannot too earnestly recall his previously expressed recommendations in relation to the establishment of a joint scientific library in Salem.

CATALOGUES.

A careful investigation has brought together one hundred and fifteen catalogues, dating from 1799 to the present time, and lists referring to the specimens in the museum; many of these are large bound volumes, while others are but temporary lists of a few pages. During the autumn all have been carefully arranged and an index to them made by Mr. Arthur R. Stone, who has also completed a card catalogue of the entire ethnological department which will be of great assistance while arranging this department and serve as a basis for an enlarged and corrected catalogue for future publication.

NEW FLOOR.

The floor of the large hall, originally laid in 1824, has never been repaired; it is nearly worn out and being of soft pine is ground to a powder by continual treading of heavy feet, which adds materially to the dust coming from other sources. This floor will have to be replaced soon, but owing to the space occupied by new cases will not be so expensive as it would have been in 1867. The cost will not be far from $400.

DISTRIBUTION OF CATALPA TREES.

In the early spring, some seventy-five hardy western Catalpa trees, from five to eight feet high, were distributed gratuitously to persons in the county who would agree to give the tree a fair trial and report the results. These trees were raised from seedlings which were sent to the Academy three years since by Mr. Robert Douglas of Illinois for trial. They were placed in a bed at the rear of the museum grounds where they grew from plants six inches high, to the size referred to above. The western Catalpa is thought to be a different species from the southern one now in cultivation here; yet, if it prove to be only a variety of the same species, having come from plants long habituated to a colder climate it cannot fail to be, for us, a more desirable tree for cultivation than the southern form. This tree is a rapid grower and the wood exceedingly durable and promises to be not only a fine tree for cultivation but one possessing a great economic value as well. As the specimens distributed went to various localities and were planted in very different soils the results will be watched with interest.

STEAM HEATING APPARATUS.

In his last report the director called attention to the great danger of having five separate fires in the museum building, and a desire was expressed by the trustees that an enquiry should be made in relation to the expense and advisability of having a steam heating apparatus placed in the building. During the year the building has been examined by an experienced mechanic and by a manufacturer of steam furnaces, whose reports are presented.

This is a matter of great importance and should of course be considered carefully, yet, in view of demands for museum room and the importance of restricting the use of the building to museum purposes and also the still greater importance of rendering it as nearly fireproof as circumstances will permit, it is a fair question to consider, whether or not, some radical measures may not be adopted to accomplish all these ends at once.

JOHN ROBINSON,
Treas. in charge of the Museum.

East India Marine Hall,
Feb. 10, 1883.

1883.

SIXTEENTH ANNUAL REPORT.

I.

REPORT OF EDW. S. MORSE, DIRECTOR.

The following report of my work for the Academy done while abroad is respectfully submitted to the trustees.

The plan which was submitted to the trustees three years ago, in which it was suggested that special attention should be given to the development of the natural history collection of Essex County and to' the development of the ethnological collections of the world, has been strictly adhered to. During my absence from the Academy Mr. Robinson has had full charge, and the present excellent condition of the collections is due to his untiring and faithful supervision of the work. The special details of this work are fully set forth in his report.

Having received a leave of absence from the trustees for the purpose of visiting Japan and China, I left Salem early in the spring of 1882 and reached Japan in May. On my arrival in that country I had several interviews with Mr. Kato, the Director of the Imperial University, and told him that my time was to be divided in collecting ethnological material for the museum of the Academy, and the study of ethnology and archæology and specially the keramic art. A suite of rooms in a little house near the astronomical observatory was fitted up for me by the University and given to me free of cost during my entire stay. Rooms and closets in other college buildings were given to me for storage purposes and, indeed, everything was done by the Japanese authorities to facilitate my work, without which assistance little progress could have been made in the task I had planned. My thanks are especially due to Prof. and Mrs. Fenollosa for many kindnesses and accommodations in connection with the objects of my work.

The collections of corals, sent out by the Academy for the Educational Museum and the University Museum, were thankfully received. Proper cases were especially built for their accommodation, and I personally superintended the mounting and arrangement of the specimens. Mr. Kuhara in charge of the museum, and Mr. Tanada rendered every assistance in this work. In return for these collections, the Educational Museum presented to the Academy a large collection of tools illustrating the trades of Japan. Great credit is due Mr. Tejima, the director of the Educational Museum, for the thorough way in which this collection was brought together. Not only were the various implements collected, but in many cases partially completed specimens of the work, as well as colored sketches, accompanied the tools.

Through the influence of Dr. W. S. Bigelow the Academy is indebted for the remarkable collection of weapons, which were presented by a famous sword merchant, Mr. Machida Heikichi.

Having explained to Mr. Machida the objects of the Academy and the nature of its museum, Mr. Machida, with great pains and at his own expense, brought together the invaluable collection of swords, spears, bows and arrows, and other weapons, which now enrich the Academy's museum, and presented them outright, properly labelled and prepared for shipment.

In the ethnological collections made for the Academy are many donations from all classes of society — professors, students, antiquarians. Even the servants and the children took special interest in giving objects to the museum, some of them of value, and all of importance.

The thanks of the Academy are especially due Dr. W. S. Bigelow, not only for numerous contributions, but also for timely aid and advice in many ways. To Mr. Takanaka Hachitaro, who was my constant companion, great credit is due for the careful way in which the Japanese names were secured for all the objects collected. He also presented many objects of household use and clothing. I would also specially mention Mr. H. Takamine, director of the Tokio Normal School, and his accomplished wife, Mr. Miyaoka Tsunejiro, the lamented Mr. Saze, Mr Tahara, Prof. Yatabe, Mr. Sasaki and many others, for kind assistance, whose names will appear in a future list of donors. To Prof. Mitsukuri thanks are due for the successful way in which the large figures were made which now adorn the museum. Prof. Mitsukuri, at great trouble, sought out the proper person to whom was intrusted the making of the figures, and personally superintended their dressing and arrangement.

Most of my time being spent in Japan but little time was given for other countries visited. In China I stopped only at Shanghai, Hong Kong and Canton. At Shanghai much help was given me by Mr. J. L. Hammond and Mr. Drew. Through Mr. Hammond I was made acquainted with Count Von Mollendorff, then on his way to Korea as special commissioner for China. I authorized him to spend a limited sum for purchases of ethnological materials in that country, and gave him a brief list of desirable objects; and a hearty acknowledgment is due him for the intelligent way in which he gratuitously carried out the commission. The results of his work, filling four large shipping cases, have already been received and unpacked. They arrived in fair condition, and as far as I know this is the first collection of Korean objects ever sent from that country. In this connection it is proper to mention that members of the Korean Embassy who visited this country last year presented a number of objects to the Academy, and one of their suite, Mr. Yu Kil Chun, who remained in this country, and who is now living in Salem, presented his entire suit of clothing and other objects to the museum.

At Hong Kong I received much assistance from Dr. Rogers and Mr. Dolan. A trip was made to Canton and beyond for purposes of collecting, and many interesting objects were secured. By taking the French mail for Singapore I had an opportunity of stopping at Saigon, in Anam, and while there visited Cholon, a few miles distant, and purchased a number of Anamese objects. At Singapore my stay was very short and only a few objects were obtained.

A hasty visit to Java, in company with Mr. J. W. Bookwalter, resulted in securing a few objects, all of which were presented by this gentleman. In China, Anam, Singapore and Java, I made special study of the houses, arrangements of fireplace, and matters concerning the disposal of sewerage. The Malay houses, resting on piles, often springing from a malarial swampy ground, make their study one of risk and discomfort. Here I became ill, and in Java by further exposure contracted an illness which rendered me nearly helpless until I reached home. I made a short stay at Marseilles, Paris, and London, but was enabled only to make the most general observations. What strength I had was given to an examination of museum arrangement, the mounting and display of specimens, etc. With the exception of the National Museum of Antiquities at St. Germain, I saw nothing in the way of cases, or methods of mounting, that we could adopt with advantage. Indeed, I was much struck with the furniture and rude methods employed. The Museum of Antiquities, however, furnished most perfect models for cases for archæological specimens.

In London, many kindnesses were shown me by Prof. Owen, Prof. Huxley, Mr. Franks, director of the British Museum, Dr. Woodward, director of the Geological department, Dr. Lancaster, of the London University, and others. Cases were unlocked and every facility given me to examine their construction.

At Liverpool, I saw the famous Free Museum, which, for excellence of arrangement and attractive methods of display, exceeds all the museums that I saw. The methods employed in mounting the collections of shells, and the plans of the cases containing them, might serve as models. Certainly, I never before saw a collection so perfectly arranged.

Strange as it may seem, but little was observed in the various museums visited that would be an improvement in our methods. And, in the matter of cases, those of the Smithsonian Institution and the American Museum of Natural History in New York are infinitely superior.

EDWARD S. MORSE, Director.
East India Marine Hall,
    Feb. 1, 1884.

II.

REPORT ON THE WORK OF THE ACADEMY AND THE CONDITION OF THE MUSEUM, FOR 1883, BY JOHN ROBINSON, TREAS. IN CHARGE.

COLLECTIONS AND ARRANGEMENTS.

The rearrangement of the collections in the exhibition hall has been steadily continued during the year. In April and May a portion of the objects from Polynesia

were placed in the new (southern) case on the eastern
side of the hall, and those from North and South America in the eastern side of the central case opposite. Following this work the general collections of mammals were
then arranged according to their proper sequence and labelled, and the birds, reptiles and fishes arranged as far as
possible. This occupied the time to June 15.

Immediately, on its arrival, the Japanese ethnological
collection was temporarily placed in the new northern
case on the eastern side of the hall. The specimens,
however, are much crowded, and more room will be required to display them properly.

A temporary arrangement has also been made of the
collections formed by Mr. Morse in Singapore, Anam,
Canton, etc., and other collections from the East, including the gifts of Mr. Dolan, Yu Kil Chun (Korean), the
specimens from Yesso and photographs from Japan.

The Essex County collection in the gallery has, with
the exception of the prehistoric relics, been rearranged,
and large additions made to the shells, birds, mammals,
plants, etc. The birds and mammals of this collection
have been cleaned and remounted on uniform stands
which has greatly improved their appearance. An addition of nearly twenty running feet of case room has also
been secured in the gallery by an alteration in the wood-
work and plastering surrounding the old chimneys.

The general collection is in better condition than ever
before. Large numbers of labels have been added to the
specimens in all departments, several wooden signs have
been placed outside of the cases and the large specimens
on the walls and surmounting the cabinets on the lower
floor have been marked with large clear labels which have
been glazed to preserve them. The jaw of the "Right"
or "Fin Back" whale has been hung over the coral case
near that of the Sperm whale.

ACCESSIONS.

The accessions to the museum have been more numerous and more valuable than during any year, perhaps
since the foundation of the E. I. M. collection in 1799.
The principal ones are as follows :—

Morse collection, Japan,	680 specimens.	
Morse collection, elsewhere,	141	"
Wm. Dolan, collection, China,	50	"
Botanical,	200	"
Other accessions,	300	"
Models of boats (large),	12	

Additions to County collections :—

Plants,	54	
Mammals,	50	
Archæology (85 lots),	322	"

(This last includes about fifteen lots, fifty specimens
outside.)

An oil painting of Capt. John Bertram by Edgar Parker,
and a smaller pastel of Capt. John Becket, Jr. (drawn
in 1811), have been presented to the E. I. M. Society
and placed in the hall.

To the library 340 numbers have been added :—
12 bound volumes by gift,
12 " " " purchase,
316 pamphlets, parts and serials by gift.

In order to make the most useful books in the library
more accessible, those seldom or never used have been
packed in boxes and stored in the attic. The library
cases have all been painted on the inside, an additional
case placed in the room, and the books all rearranged.

PUBLICATIONS.

By an arrangement with the publisher, a special edition

of "Abbott's Primitive Industry" was printed for the Academy. A copy was sent to every foreign correspondent who has sent us publications and a copy placed in some library in nearly every town in Essex County. As this work is based very largely upon specimens in our museum it was a very desirable publication for distribution.

One thousand copies of the "Salem Gazette," containing the last report of the museum and list of accessions for the year, were distributed in Essex County and to persons at a distance likely to be interested in the matter it contained and, at each quarter of the year the "Gazette" now publishes an account of the general work at the museum and a list of accessions, which is forwarded to each donor. This has in a marked way increased the number of local accessions.

Mr. C. S. Sargent gave the Academy, for distribution in the county, 100 copies of "Scudder's Pine Moth," a pamphlet of twenty pages, and one lithographic (colored) plate. This moth has made sad havoc among the pines on the island of Nantucket and it is desirable that information relating to it should reach the owners of pine woodlands.

The publication of a "Pocket Guide to Salem" gave an opportunity to publish a more carefully prepared account of the Academy, its work and collections, than has heretofore appeared. Thousands of this little guide have been sold and distributed by its publishers.

A card has also been prepared for distribution stating, briefly, the points in the history of the Academy, the nature of the collections, list of officers, etc. These are given to visitors from a distance and serve to answer the numerous questions which are always asked by strangers.

LECTURES, ETC.

The two courses of lectures arranged for the summer school in 1882 were delivered in January and February; Mr. J. W. Fewkes giving five on Corals and Coral Islands, and Prof. C. E. Bessey three on Physiological Botany. The lectures were given in Plummer Hall and were attended by upwards of 200 persons, including many teachers.

Mr. Sears' botanical class was continued into June with an average attendance of twelve persons; twenty-four lessons were given. The botanical section for more advanced study held eleven meetings, with an average attendance of eighteen persons, taking for a subject the "structure of Vascular Cryptogams."

Mr. Sears has spoken at Swampscott and Danvers before local clubs and at Institute meetings, and the present writer at Swampscott and at Institute meetings at Rowley and Plummer Hall, both appearing as part of their Academy work, and speaking on local collecting and botanical study.

VISITORS.

36,056 persons have visited the museum during the year. The greatest number on single days were : —

Feb. 22,	440.
April 5 (Fast day),	346.
Sept. 25 (first day of cattle show),	384.
Sept. 26 (second day of cattle show),	936.
Nov. 29 (Thanksgiving),	336.
July 4,	182.

July 4 is mentioned to show how few persons visit the museum on holidays now as compared with such days in former years, especially in the summer when "attractions" are offered at the "Willows," "Point of Pines," and other popular resorts in the neighborhood. The above figures, showing the total number of visitors, are undoubtedly under the actual numbers. There is a steady increase each year of late, in the regular daily attendance and a corresponding decrease on popular holidays.

The specimens which seem to be of most interest to the public are the life-size figures from China, Japan, India, etc., the general collection of mammals and birds, the Essex County animals and woods and, perhaps more than anything else, the human skeletons and crania. The carving, "Heaven and the Day of Judgment," of course holds the first place for the seeker after the curious and wonderful.

It has been found necessary to limit the age of children admitted without a guardian to fourteen years, all under that age being excluded; this undoubtedly reduces the total number of visitors by 1000, yet the number for the year is about the same as for 1882.

The museum has been visited by the Malagassy envoys, the Korean embassy, and by many distinguished persons sojourning in this neighborhood, including several English gentlemen of note. The teachers from Rockport and the High School children from that town passed an afternoon at the Museum, and several other schools and visiting organizations have made unannounced calls.

The visitors from the county have been more numerous than ever before, over 1200 persons from the towns of Essex County visiting the hall during the days the Agricultural Society held its annual fair at the "Willows."

JOHN ROBINSON.

East India Marine Hall,
Feb. 1, 1884.

AN ACCOUNT

OF THE

SUMMER SCHOOL OF BIOLOGY

1876----1881.

WITH LISTS OF THE

LECTURERS AND STUDENTS.

SUMMER SCHOOL OF BIOLOGY.

Early in the spring of 1876 Dr. Packard, then director of the Academy, proposed the establishment of a Summer School of Biology modelled after Prof. Agassiz's school at Penekese which Dr. Packard had attended as a lecturer. This proposition was favored by the trustees, and the director and treasurer were authorized to perfect the arrangements. A lecture room was fitted up in East India Marine Hall and, upon the land in the rear, a laboratory was built 30 by 20 in which suitable tables and black boards were placed; small tables around the room for students and a long one in the centre for aquaria and large dissections. In response to a circular issued, calling attention to the school and giving a list of lecturers, sixteen students appeared at the opening of the session, July 7, 1876. The school continued successfully for seven years conducted mainly upon the original plan. The following lists give the names of the lecturers, their subjects and the students attending the summer school for the seven years it was continued.

1876.

LECTURERS AND SUBJECTS.

Prof. E. S. Morse, ten on Zoölogy and Evolution.
Mr. John Robinson, ten on Botany.
Rev. E. C. Bolles, six on Microscopy.
Dr. A. S. Packard, seven on Zoölogy.
Dr. A. H. Johnson, four on Physiology.
Mr. J. S. Kingsley, two on Crustacea.

STUDENTS.

Miss M. E. Stanley, Salem, Mass.

Mrs. George C. Fitch, Grand Rapids, Mich.
Miss Mary T. Saunders, Salem, Mass.
Miss E. W. Beaman, Amherst, Mass.
Miss Hannah E. Burke, Beverly, Mass.
Miss M. B. Smith, Beverly, Mass.
Miss Elizabeth Thurber, Plymouth, Mass.
Miss Lucia Bartlett, Plymouth, Mass.
Mrs. Marie L. Walker, Washington, D. C.
Miss Cora H. Clarke, Boston, Mass.
Miss Emily A. Glover, Salem, Mass.
Miss Susan M. Hallowell, Wellesley, Mass.
Mr. W. P. Conant, Wenham, Mass.
Mr. Leslie A. Lee, Franklin, Mass.
Mr. Arthur F. Gray, Danvers, Mass.
Mr. Henry Priest, Barre, N. H.

1877.

LECTURERS AND SUBJECTS.

Mr. J. H. Emerton, eight on Zoölogy and six on Spiders and allied forms.

Dr. A. S. Packard, eight on Insects.

Mr. J. S. Kingsley, three on Crustacea.

Prof. R. Ramsay Wright, one on Sponges and seven on Vertebrates.

Dr. C. S. Minot, six on General Histology.

Rev. E. C. Bolles, six on Microscopy.

Mr. John Robinson, four on Botany.

Rev. A. B. Hervey, two on Algæ.

STUDENTS.

Miss Mary V. Lee, M. D., Oswego, N. Y.
Miss Susan M. Hallowell, Wellesley, Mass.
Miss C. C. Haskell, Poughkeepsie, N. Y.
Miss M. E. Stanley, Salem, Mass.

Miss M. C. Jackson, Beverly Farms, Mass.

Miss Sophia Locher, Poughkeepsie, N. Y.

Miss Hannah E. Burke, Beverly, Mass.

Miss Margarette W. Brooks, Salem, Mass.

Miss Mary J. Studley, M. D., So. Framingham, Mass.

Miss Cornelia F. Morris, Syracuse, N. Y.

Mrs. K. T. Woods, Salem, Mass.

Mr. Otto H. Schulte, So. Williamstown, Mass.

Mr. Takamine, Oswego, N. Y. (Japan).

Mr. Krusi, Oswego, N. Y.

Rev. W. J. Parrot, Jackson, Mich.

Mr. J. H. Haynes, Williamstown, Mass.

Mr. S. T. Moreland, Baltimore, Md.

Mr. Edw. B. Sanger, Ithaca, N. Y.

Mr. Frederick Starr, Auburn, N. Y.

Mr. Herbert B. Preston, Lexington, Va.

Mr. Joseph H. Horton, Ipswich, Mass.

[Seven others attended the lectures only.]

1878.

LECTURERS AND SUBJECTS.

Dr. A. S. Packard, fourteen on Zoölogy.

Dr. C. S. Minot, five on Vertebrates and six on General Histology.

Mr. J. H. Emerton, six on Spiders and allied forms.

Rev. E. C. Bolles, five on Microscopy.

Mr. J. S. Kingsley, two on Crustacea.

STUDENTS.

Mr. S. M. Ward, Ellensville, N. Y.

Mr. Wm. Griffen, Lynn, Mass.

Mr. Lucius Hubbard, So. Bend, Ind.

Mr. F. H. Parsons.

Rev. S. M. Newman, Taunton, Mass.

Mr. Austin Garver, Greenwood, Mass.
Mr. E. S. Gardner.
Dr. H. C. Bolton, Hartford, Conn.
Mr. Justin Spaulding.
Mr. Willard Sanborn.
Mr. J. T. Holt.
Miss Eliza Talcott.
Miss Morrison.

1879.

LECTURES AND INSTRUCTION.

Mr. J. H. Emerton gave the lectures and instruction at a temporary laboratory at the " Willows."

STUDENTS.

Miss Sela Wilson.
Miss Burke.
Prof. S. Calvin, State Univ. Iowa, Iowa City, Iowa.
Prof. T. H. McBride, State Univ. Iowa, Iowa City, Iowa.
Mr. Andrew Nichols, Danvers, Mass.

1880.

LECTURERS AND SUBJECTS.

Mr. J. W. Fewkes, six on the Lower Invertebrates.
Dr. Geo. L. Goodale, seven on Vegetable Physiology.
Dr. Geo. M. Sternberg, two on Anatomy and Germs.
Prof. E. S. Morse, fifteen on Zoölogy.
Mr. Chas. Fish, seven on Insects.
Mr. John Robinson, four on Cryptogamic Botany.
Prof. H. H. Straight, six on Vertebrates.

STUDENTS.

Mrs. Geo. M. Sternberg, Kentucky.
Miss Annie L. Page, Danvers, Mass.

Miss J. A. Fielding, Wallingford, Conn.
Miss Judith W. Bartlett, East Salisbury, Mass.
Miss E. Josephine Roach, Danvers, Mass.
Miss M. Burke, Pittsfield, Mass.
Miss ·Jennie Pindell, Baltimore, Md. .
Miss Laura P. Stone, Newton, Mass.
Miss Margarette W. Brooks, Salem, Mass.
Dr. Geo. M. Sternberg, U.S.A.
Prof. C. W. Hall, Univ. Minn., Minneapolis, Minn.
Mr. R. P. Williams, Newton, Mass.
Mr. Edwin S. Hallock, Glen Cove, L. I., N. Y.
Mr. H. Saze, Tokio, Japan.
[Eight others attended the lectures only].

1881.

LECTURERS AND SUBJECTS.

Mr. J. W. Fewkes, six on the Lower Invertebrates.
Mr. Chas. Fish, seven on Insects.
Prof. E. S. Morse, eleven on Zoölogy and Evolution.
Prof. H. H. Straight, seven on Vertebrates.
Prof. Penhallow, three on Botany.
Dr. C. S. Minot, seven on Embryology.

STUDENTS.

Miss Anna L. Page, Danvers, Mass.
Miss E. Josephine Roach, Danvers, Mass.
Miss Jenny Lynch, Minnesota.
Miss Bessie W. Eaton, Salem, Mass.
Miss Margarette W. Brooks, Salem, Mass.
Miss Fanny D. Chamberlain, Buffalo, N. Y.

In the work of the Summer School, the Academy received the hearty support of many friends. Several of
the lecturers gave their services. Among such were Rev.

E. C. Bolles, Prof. E. S. Morse, Rev. A. B. Hervey, Dr. A. H. Johnson, Mr. J. S. Kingsley, Mr. John Robinson and, later, Prof. R. Ramsay Wright and Dr. Geo. M. Sternberg. The Academy was also indebted to Mr. T. F. Hunt of Salem for continued and liberal contributions to the support of the school.

In 1881, however, it became evident that the object for which the school was organized had not been fully realized, viz., the instruction of Essex County teachers; for, although the maximum number of students which could be accommodated had been often reached, yet, but few persons from the county had attended the school during its continuance. Added to this, schools of similar character had been established in the western and middle states thereby lessening the number attending from those regions, and the feeling had justly gained ground that many teachers were overtaxing themselves during a season which should properly be given up to rest and recuperation.

It was therefore decided, unless ten students were secured for the session proposed for 1882, that the school should be abandoned. This number was not reached and the term was given up for the year. Of the lecturers who had been engaged, two consented to deliver their lectures during the winter of 1882–3 before audiences of teachers and others. These courses were given by Prof. C. E. Bessey who delivered four lectures on Physiological Botany and Dr. J. W. Fewkes who delivered six lectures on Corals and Coral Islands. These lectures were attended by an audience of 200 persons mostly teachers and students in the higher grade schools. This closed the work of the Summer School of the Academy which, although having continued but seven years, outlived many similar schools.

PEABODY ACADEMY OF SCIENCE.

SEVENTEENTH

ANNUAL REPORT.

MUSEUM REPORTS; FINANCIAL STATEMENT; ACCESSIONS TO THE MUSEUM AND LIBRARY FOR 1884. PROCEEDINGS OF THE TRUSTEES AT THE ANNUAL MEETING, FEBRUARY 18, 1885.

SALEM:

PRINTED FOR THE ACADEMY.

1885.

(67)

PROCEEDINGS OF THE TRUSTEES.

Feb. 18, 1885. (Ninetieth anniversary of the birth of George Peabody.)

Annual meeting of the Trustees at 7.30 P. M. Present: the President, Vice President, Secretary, Treasurer and Messrs. Cogswell and Peabody.

The report of the Treasurer was read and accepted.

The report of the Director was read; the condensed annual reports since 1874, ordered to be prepared at the last annual meeting, were presented and Mr. Robinson read his report on the condition of the Museum. These reports were accepted. The following officers were unanimously chosen by ballot:

WILLIAM C. ENDICOTT, *President.*
HENRY WHEATLAND, *Vice President.*
ABNER C. GOODELL, JR., *Secretary.*
JOHN ROBINSON, *Treasurer.*

Finance Committee: the President, Treasurer and Dr. Cogswell.

Executive Committee: the President, Vice President, Secretary, Treasurer and Dr. Nichols. On motion of Dr. Wheatland, Mr. Arthur R. Stone was appointed assistant at the Museum. On motion of Dr. Wheatland it was voted that all unprinted reports be printed forthwith.

The appropriations for the year were voted and the subject of the addition to the East India Marine Hall was fully discussed, plans examined and estimates considered.

The board then adjourned.

Attest,   A. C. GOODELL, JR., *Secretary.*

Report of the Treasurer of the Peabody Academy

Dr.   CASH.

1884.

Jan. 31. To Balance of account this date	$13,551 07	
" Rec'd for Cincinnati, Sandusky & Cleveland R. R. Bonds, drawn	1,000 00	$14,551 07

Receipts for the year ending January 31, 1885.

Rents Museum Building	575 00	
" King do	1,870 00	
" Hubon do	390 00	
" Cook do	264 00	
Receipts for Coupons Indianapolis & Vincennes R. R.	700 00	
" " " Del. & Hudson Canal Co.	280 00	
" " " Mobile & Ohio R. R. . .	300 00	
" " " Chicago City	700 00	
" " " Michigan Central R. R. .	400 00	
" " " Scioto Valley R. R. . .	350 00	
" " " Kansas City, St. Jo & C. Bluffs R. R. . . .	350 00	
" " " Chicago & E. Illinois R. R. .	180 00	
" " " Cincinnati, Sandusky and Cleveland R. R. . . .	570 00	
" " Dividends Salem Nat. Bank . .	300 00	
" " " Fort Wayne & Jackson R. R.	363 00	
" " Interest on Mortgage note . . .	270 00	
" " " Salem Nat. Bank . . .	327 08	
" " Tax returned on Bank stock . .	195 03	

Receipts at Museum.			
Bird account	269 55		
E. A. Snow	10 27		
Sundries sold	31 06	310 88	$ 8,694 99
			$23,246 06

To Balance brought forward 1,881 24

                           JOHN ROBINSON,

SALEM, JANUARY 31, 1885.   *Treasurer.*

of Science of Salem for the year ending January 31, 1885.

CASH.

Investments for the year ending January 31, 1885.

By paid King Building Improvement . . .	$3,300 00
" " $5,000 Burlington Cedar Rapids and North-	
ern R. R. Bonds, 50 yrs., 5 per cent. .	4,595 83
" " 50 shares Chicago, Burlington and Quincy	
Railroad	6,131 25
	$14,027 08

Expenditures for the year ending January 31, 1885.

By paid Salaries and clerk hire at Museum .	$3,878 00	
" " Permanent additions to furniture, cases,		
etc., at Museum	827 00	
" " Permanent additions to Museum spec-		
imens	675 00	
" " Books and Binding	117 00	
" " Other Museum expenses	815 60	
		$ 5,782 60

" " State, County and City tax	528 50	
" " City of Salem water tax	46 35	
" " Bookkeeper and care of real estate . .	300 00	
" " King Building repairs	196 63	
" " Hubon House repairs	11 09	
" " Cook House repairs	15 62	
" " Museum Building repairs	436 95	
" " Safe Box rent	20 00	1,555 14
Balance to new acct.		1,881 24
		$23,246 60

Property Statement.*

Permanent Fund, January 31, 1885,	$100,000.00
Reserve Fund, January 31, 1885,	14,306.70
	$114,306.70

Invested as Follows.

10,000	City of Chicago Water Loan Bonds 7 per cent, due 1894,	$9,547 22
10,000	Indianapolis & Vincennes R.R. Bonds 7 per cent, due 1908,	8,500 00
9,000	Cincinnati, Sandusky & Cleveland R.R. B'ds 6 per cent, due 1900,	9,348 84
5,000	Michigan Central R.R. Bonds 8 per cent, due 1890,	5,410 00
5,000	Scioto Valley Railroad Bonds 7 per cent, due 1896,	5,164 30
5,000	Kansas City, St. Jo. & C. Bluffs R.R. Bonds 7 per cent, due 1907,	5,490 31
5,000	Burlington, Cedar Rapids & No. R.R. Bonds 5 per cent, due 1934	4,595 83
5,000	Mobile & Ohio Railroad Bonds 6 per cent, due 1891,	5,189 08
4,000	Delaware & Hudson Canal Co. Bonds 7 per cent, due 1917,	4,040 88
3,000	Chicago & Eastern Illinois R.R. Bonds 6 per cent, due 1907,	3,007 33
50 shares	Salem National Bank of Salem,	5,944 86
50 "	Chicago, Burlington & Quincy R.R.,	6,131 25
66 "	Fort Wayne & Jackson Railroad,	4,605 56
	F. W. Putnam's mortgage note,	4,500 00
	King Building, Essex St., Salem,	25,800 00
	Hubon House, Charter St, "	3,000 00
	Cook House, " "	2,200 00
	Deposit Salem National Bank,	1,881 24
		$114,306 70

* Not including the East India Marine Hall property, museum fittings, furniture, library nor collections, which, exclusive of the collections received as permanent deposits from the East India Marine Soc. and Essex Inst., may be roughly estimated at upwards of $50,000.

MUSEUM REPORTS.

I.

REPORT OF EDWARD S. MORSE, DIRECTOR.

The Director would respectfully submit to the Trustees of the Peabody Academy of Science the following report for the year 1884.

The progress made in the arrangement of the several collections; the accessions to the Museum and library; the various improvements effected in the building, and many other details connected with the work during the past year, are very fully and clearly set forth in the report of Mr. John Robinson, Treasurer, in charge of the Museum. This report will indicate to the Trustees the progress made in the general work of the Museum and the increasing favor this progress meets with from the public as indicated, not only in the number, but in the character of the visitors who daily frequent the halls of the Academy.

For many years the Peabody Academy of Science has had in its keeping a large and miscellaneous collection of insects. This collection contained many valuable types described by Dr. A. S. Packard, a former Director of the Museum, as well as a large amount of material brought together through his connection with the Academy. Until within a few years the Academy had among its officers special entomologists whose duty it was to look after these collections. As is well known, there is no department requiring more constant and painstaking care than the preservation of a collection of insects. So long as the Academy had in its employ trained entomologists like Dr. Packard and Mr. Emerton, but little difficulty was experienced in the proper preservation of these specimens. On the assumption of his duties by the present Director in 1880 a definite plan of work was arranged and submitted to the Trustees, which met with their approval. This plan briefly set forth the necessity of limiting for the present the work of the Academy to increasing its unrivalled ethnological collections and the perfecting the collections of animals and plants of Essex County, thus broadly covering the main objects of the two collections that had been merged together, namely, those of the East India Marine Society and of the Essex Institute. The success of this in the four years since its adoption has been so apparent that no deviation has been made. The proper carrying out of this scheme not only absorbed the limited resources of the Academy but demanded the undivided attention of those engaged in the work. The Academy not having in its employ any one specially trained as an entomologist, great difficulty was experienced in guarding the large collection of insects in its possession. Indeed, with what care it had been able to bestow upon them, they were not only in a perilous condition but their value was rapidly deteriorating from year to year. It was at last realized that unless immediate and constant attention was given them they would meet with the fate of similar collections in other museums of the country. Knowing that the Museum of Comparative Zoölogy was properly equipped with men and means necessary to the care of such material, it was hoped that some arrangement could be made whereby these collections might be preserved in the best interests of Science. The Director communicated with Mr. Agassiz in regard to the matter and he finally consented to take them under the protecting care of that institution. Having consulted with the executive committee, and getting their approval, the collections, which in spite of what care could be given them were rapidly going to ruin, have been transferred without conditions to the Museum at Cambridge. In return the Academy will receive from time to time collections of animals necessary to perfect the typical collections of animals now being placed on permanent exhibition. Thus will be preserved and utilized for science, collections which, despite all precautions, would have deteriorated from year to year.

That this step has been a wise one is attested by the commendations of entomologists, who looked with grave alarm at the hazardous condition of these objects in past years.

The plans for the extension of the building have been submitted to the building committee and have met with its approval. Work, however, cannot be commenced upon it until the northern boundary of this building is definitely determined upon. When this point is finally settled there is no reason why the work should not be immediately commenced. The Director would earnestly recommend, that in any plan for the heating of this new portion some provision may be made for the partial heating, at least, of the present exhibition hall. Despite the fact that the Museum is opened during the winter the cold is often so intense that its halls are at times deserted and active work on the collections is rendered impossible.

The record of the daily number of visitors at the Museum is a matter of importance, not only as indicating the interest taken in its work by the public, but showing from year to year a marked increase in this number. The present mode of enumerating these visitors is obviously imperfect and the Director would suggest that some method be provided by which an accurate count can be made from day to day, methods similar to those employed in the larger museums abroad as well as in some of our institutions in this country.

It is a matter of congratulation that the shop in the Museum building has been finally vacated, for though the occupant, Mr. T. B. Nichols, had been an esteemed and careful tenant, nevertheless there were grounds for anxiety in the presence of material recognized as hazardous.

The liberal provision made for the Director in the disposal of the greater portion of his time in the preparation of his work on Japan, has been fully utilized by him in the work of preparing the text as well as of the drawings to illustrate it. Arrangements have been made with the publishers whereby the Academy will receive at cost price a certain number of copies for exchange with its correspondents abroad.

EDWARD S. MORSE.

East India Marine Hall,
Feb. 10, 1885.

II.

REPORT ON THE WORK OF THE ACADEMY AND THE CONDITION OF THE MUSEUM WITH LISTS OF ACCESSIONS TO THE MUSEUM AND LIBRARY.

BY JOHN ROBINSON, TREASURER, IN CHARGE OF THE MUSEUM.

It will be seen by my last report that the work for the year 1883 consisted principally in the rearrangement of the specimens in the exhibition cases of the Museum. During the year 1884 this work has been steadily continued, so that, now, the entire collection has been rearranged in accordance with the plan recommended by Mr. Morse when he entered upon his duties as Director in 1880. It should be understood, however, that this general work has been preliminary in its nature, as almost every day something is suggested by which it may be improved in minor ways and made more instructive to visitors and students. When the changes were completed, which required the objects to be moved from case to case, the work of labelling the specimens was begun, the larger portion of my time for three months being devoted to this work. For the labels, manila tag stock of the best quality was used, such as has been adopted by the National Museum in Washington. Labels of this sort are inexpensive, less glaring to the eyes and, being of a buff tint at first, have the great advantage of not becoming yellow by age and hence disfiguring the collections, as labels written upon white paper do in the course of two or three years.

The collections rearranged during the year were those from Korea, Japan and India. Those which have been fully labelled in addition to these are the collections from Africa, Arabia, Polynesia, and North and South America.

As circumstances permitted, work has been continued upon the zoölogical collections and although the arrangement of the type collection in the Museum is not yet completed, but two important gaps remain and these are to be filled by representatives of the mollusks and the insects. Specimens for the section of mollusks are now being mounted and provision is being made for the insects. Much less work has been done on the Essex County collection than during the two previous years as the specimens were already arranged as well as the space allotted to them would permit. They require however to be relabelled and this can be done another season.

A careful examination has been made of the records and the early manuscript catalogues of the East India Marine Society and all matters of interest and dates relating to the ethnological specimens of the Museum have been added to the card catalogue of that collection. In this way many errors have been corrected and many facts of scientific value have been associated with the specimens themselves. In addition to the work on the collections which are now on public exhibition good progress has been made upon the others. The specimens of mollusca, a large portion of which have never been unpacked from the boxes which contained them in 1867, have been assorted into families and temporarily placed in a new storage case of one hundred and sixty-eight trays built for this purpose in the attic. The portion of the collection which was arranged and mounted upon tablets by Mr. Cooke in 1877-80 has been placed in a suitable case of one hundred and twenty trays in the lecture room where it has been assorted into families and some additions made to it from the specimens in the attic. To this collection will be added, as the specimens can be compared family by family, all which are required to complete it from the storage cases. As an interest has of late developed in the collecting of shells by many young people in this neighborhood it is important that the collection should be in such condition as to afford them means for naming and arranging their specimens. The collection owned by the Academy is a very fine one and when properly arranged will take a high rank among similar collections in this country.

Another department which has until recently received but little attention is that of Mineralogy. During the year a storage case of ninety trays has been built in the cellar and a portion of the minerals and geological specimens roughly sorted in it. In the fall an arrangement was made with the Rev. Benj. F. McDaniel of Salem by which he has kindly agreed to look over these collections and select from them such specimens as ought to be preserved for the cabinet when the time shall arrive to arrange them. It is intended also to make such use of the duplicates for exchanges or class work as will be for the best advantage of the Academy.

In the department of Botany a great improvement has been made. As various collections were from time to time mounted, they were placed in boxes in the dark spare room on the lower floor of the museum. This year a suitable herbarium case of white wood containing ninety six compartments has been placed in the lecture room in which all the Essex County collections and the general reference collection from North America have been arranged. Other collections have also been placed in the lecture room so that, now, the herbarium is in a dry and pleasant room where it can be easily referred to by those in charge of it and by students who desire to consult it.

The Academy now owns a very good collection of botanical reference books and two microscopes which are placed at the disposal of any persons desiring to compare species at the museum. The herbarium is by far the best in the county. It is centrally and conveniently situated and has been frequently consulted through the year by students in this department of study. The special work on this collection has been the arrangement of the Algae, of which there were a large number of specimens. These have been named and classified by Mr. Frank S. Collins of Malden, a special student of this group of plants. This gentleman has also added many desirable species which were new to the collection. For the county collection alone we obtained from him nearly one hundred species collected in the region about Nahant and Marblehead. The Academy has also received by gift the valuable collection of Mrs. Abbie L. Davis of Gloucester. This collection is the result of many years of intelligent and patient work. Mr. Sears has also collected during the season a large number of specimens of flowering plants to add to and improve the county herbariun.

In addition to the work on the special departments of the Museum much has been done to improve the general condition of many of the specimens in the exhibition room by remounting and cleaning them. The specimens stored in the attic and cellar have been examined and in many cases repacked and assorted. Many labels have been added and large signs placed on the cases so that visitors may be able to examine the collections in serial order.

IMPROVEMENTS IN THE BUILDING.

The condition of the stairway leading to the Museum, always in a dark corner and boxed in by partitions, has been much improved by cutting away the walls and placing a neat baluster and rail in their stead. This change has not only added greatly to the appearance of the hallway, but renders the gaslight heretofore required in the afternoon unnecessary. The cellar has been whitewashed throughout, a cement floor laid over a large portion of it, and other improvements made to secure more light and better ventilation.

ACCESSIONS TO THE MUSEUM.

The accessions to the Museum for the year number three hundred and eight separate entries from one hundred and ninety-four individuals and institutions and aggregate about four thousand six hundred specimens distributed as follows:

Korean collection,	225.
Ethnological (elsewhere),	119.
Botanical specimens, Essex County,	350.
Botanical specimens (elsewhere), about	800.

Prehistoric relics, Essex County,   2,486.
Prehistoric relics (elsewhere),   32.
Zoölogical specimens, Essex County, about   100.
Miscellaneous accessions, about   500.

The list of accessions to the museum (see page 85) specifies in detail all that have been received during the year. Some, however, are of such a character as to deserve a more extended notice. These include the collections of algæ referred to elsewhere from Mr. Collins and Mrs. Davis, mounted specimens of Essex County fishes from Dr. E. H. Davidson and Mr. E. L. Wonson, specimens of Lemurs from Madagascar given by Mr. Frank H. Pitman, ethnological specimens from Africa from Mr. Harry A. Hall, two black bears from Mr. Milton A. Hammond, a Japanese shrine from Mr. Eneas Yamada and extensive additions to the local collections of prehistoric relics from Messrs. O. C. and Joseph Willcomb of Ipswich, Isaiah Dodge of Beverly and others. The collection of Korean objects received through Count Von Mollendorff, referred to in the report of the Director for 1883, arrived at the beginning of the year. The selections proved quite satisfactory, as the collection fairly represents the objects of domestic use of the common people of Korea.

PORTRAITS.

Two portraits have been received during the year as gifts to the East India Marine Society, one of James Buffington Briggs and the other of Thomas Ruee, members of that society. An effort is being made to add to this collection of portraits and also to obtain likenesses of all those who have been connected with the East India Marine Society or the Academy since the organization of these institutions.

LIBRARY.

The accessions to the library have been of the same character as heretofore, and aggregate in all three hundred and eighty-four numbers from one hundred and sixteen individuals and institutions, as follows:

Bound volumes,	40.
Parts of volumes and pamphlets,	280.
Miscellaneous papers, etc.,	64.

During the year a new catalogue of the library has been made, arranged alphabetically by places, one volume for American and one for foreign publications and showing the entire accessions since the formation of the Academy. This catalogue is now continued by transferring the entries from the book of daily accessions.

PUBLICATIONS.

The Academy has issued no publications during the year excepting circulars in relation to the collections and the quarterly and annual reports which have, as formerly, been printed gratuitously by the proprietors of the Salem Gazette. These reports have been sent to each person making a contribution to the Academy and to others likely to be interested.

LECTURES AND CLASS WORK.

The botanical section met each week in the early months of 1884, taking up the study of algæ. The attendance, as before, was good, averaging about seventeen at each meeting. A class in elementary botany was to have been conducted in the Spring, but, owing to the sickness of Mr. Sears, it was given up. A class in mineralogy and geology, under the instruction of Rev. Benj. F. McDaniel, was begun in December; the tickets, limited to twenty, were taken at once, thus proving the desire for classes in this branch of science.

VISITORS.

The visitors to the museum for the year numbered 38,251 against 36,056 in 1883, a gain of 2,195. Arranged by quarters the numbers are as follows:

	1884.	1883.
Jan. 1, to March 31,	7,822	7,575.
April 1, to June 30,	8,129	8,521.
July 1, to September 30,	13,796	12,449.
October 1, to December 31,	8,504	7,511.

The largest numbers on single days were:

Feb. 22,	467.
April 4 (Fast Day),	100.
May 30,	312.
July 1 (Barnum's circus in Salem),	456.
July 4,	432.
Sept. 22 and 23 (Cattle show at the "Willows," Salem),	536.
Oct. 23 (Meeting of the American Missionary Association in Salem),	269.
Nov. 28 (Thanksgiving day),	340.

The same gratifying results are noticed this year as last in relation to the attractiveness of the present arrangement of the collections; the daily number of visitors has not only increased but a longer time is spent by them in the hall in examining the specimens.

Since the first of May the hall has been kept open during the noon hour. This accommodates many persons who would otherwise be prevented from visiting the museum. Under this arrangement about one thousand persons entered the hall between twelve and one o'clock from May 1 to Dec. 31. Among the visitors this year there have been a larger number of persons from abroad than formerly. This class is increasing every year, the majority being English travellers. By special arrangement several parties have visited the Museum, including the members of the Groveland Flower Club, Gloucester High School, Miss Packard's private school from Lawrence and the teachers of the Bradford Academy and, as usual, many parties have made unannounced visits.

The work of the year has proceeded in a very harmonious and steady manner. As the corps of workers is small, each one is called upon to perform work of all kinds when more than one person is needed and, although it often seems from week to week, that a small amount is done, yet, in the end, much work appears to have been accomplished. Mr. Sears was necessarily absent from the Museum in the spring for nearly three months, being confined to the house by a severe sickness, and during this time Mr. Arthur R. Stone filled his place in a very satisfactory manner. I desire also to mention the faithful services of the janitor, Mr. J. R. Treadwell, who has done all the minor carpenter work, painting, etc., about the building, and that required for the arrangement of the collections. In short, those employed at the Museum have shown that interest in their work which is the surest guarantee of satisfactory results.

Respectfully submitted,

JOHN ROBINSON, Treas.,

in charge of the Museum.

East India Marine Hall,
Salem, Jan., 1885.

ACCESSIONS TO THE MUSEUM.

1884.

Almy, Jas. F., Salem. Japanese temple gong.

Andrews, Jas. M., Beverly Farms. Indian implements.

Babcock, Edw. M., Salem. Night heron, Salem Mill Pond.

Bartlett, John W., Marblehead. Cocoon of insect.

Bates, Capt. Wm. B., Salem. Spider.

Bettis, John B., Salem. *Actias Luna*, Salem.

Bigelow, Dr. W. S., Tokio, Japan. Two figures of Japanese warriors.

Blake, Joseph, Andover. Dried plants from Andover.

Blood, E. H., Lynn. Arrow points from Greenville Co., S. C.

Bolles, Rev. E. C., Salem. Sphynx moth.

Boutwell, Miss Abby E., Fitchburg, Mass. Crow Indian scalp taken in battle and worn as a decoration.

Briggs, John C., Salem. Jute in different stages of manufacture, knives used in cutting it, etc.

Brooks, H. M., Salem. Old newspaper notices of museum.

Brooks, Mrs. H. M., Salem. India cloth, etc.

Browne, Aug. S., Salem. Shark's head from Nantucket.

Burchstead, Benj. E., Wenham. Black snake.

Burton, A. R., Littleton, N. H. Photograph of Indian carving, ancient bank bills and newspaper.

Buttrick, S. B., Salem. Insects and wasp's nest.

Cabot, John, Lawrence. Collection of birds' eggs.

Carlton, Albert, Peabody. Pupæ of *Meredon.*

Castelhun, Dr. Carl, Newburyport, Mass. Essex County plants.

Chadwell, Harry, Salem. Cards with figures of economic plants.

Chadwick, Dr. J. R., Boston. Silver ore.

Chapple, Wm. F., Salem. Water scorpion from Salem.

Chase, Geo., Salem. Pampas grass.

Clark, Marietta, Topsfield. Nests and eggs of robin, red-winged blackbird and least fly-catcher.

Cloutman, **W. R.**, Salem.   Galena, dendrites, etc.

Collins, F. S., Malden.   Two hundred specimens of Algæ.

Cullen, Willie, Plum Island.   Indian implements.

Curtis, Geo. W., Topsfield.   Two otters from Middleton.

Curtis, Francis, Topsfield.   Giant puff-ball.

Davidson, Dr. H. E., Boston.   Twenty-eight specimens of fishes.

Davis, Mrs. A. L., Gloucester, Mass.   Collection of algæ, four hundred and twenty specimens.

Dennis, Edith L., Salem.   *Atticus secropia.*

Dickinson, Mrs. S. B., Ipswich, Mass.   Shells and lichens from Ipswich.

Dodge, Andrew N., Beverly, Mass.   Fungus on quince.

Dodge, Isaiah H., No. Beverly.   Collection Indian relics, almanacs, California cucumbers, etc.

Evans, Jas. A., Salem.   Indian implement.

Farney, H. F., Cincinnati, O.   Two Indian mats from British Columbia.

Faxon, Edwin, Jamaica Plain.   Mosses from Essex County.

Fisher, Chas. H., Salem.   Tile from Great Wall, China.

Fisk, Mrs. John, Salem.   Picture of ship Prudent.

Fitzgerald, Richard, Salem.   Flint concretions dug up in Charter Street.

Foote, A. E., Philadelphia, Penn.   Grass dress of Yagna Indians.

Fowler, Sam'l P., Danvers, Mass.   Specimen of *Rana* sp.

French, Arthur B., Boston, Mass.   Photograph of Temple at Nikko, Japan.

Fuller, Calvin W., Topsfield.   Borer in wood.

Gardner, Wm. F., Salem.   African axe brought home by Capt. Collins Ingalls about 1830.

Getchell, J. B., Salem.   Stone from drift gravel.

Goldsmith, Capt. John, Salem.   Native cloths from Ashantee and Dahomey countries, Africa.

Goodridge, Miss C. E., Salem.   Abnormal *Rudbeckia hirta.*

Goss, F. P., Salem.   Ancient wrought nails.

Gould, A. A., Peabody, Mass.   Iron pyrites, Rowe, Mass.

Gould, Miss Susie, Topsfield.   Hornet's nest, stone Indian relic and abnormal apple blossom.

Gould, Walter F., Ipswich, Mass. Crested cormorant from Ipswich.

Grant, J. W., Salem. Wood bored by Toredo.

Gray, Arthur F., Danvers, Mass. Great horned owls from Nebraska.

Greey, Edward, N. Y. City, N. Y. Japanese saddle and stirrups.

Hall, Harry A., Chelsea, Mass. Ethnological specimens from Africa.

Hammond, Milton A., Ellensburgh, N. Y. Large female black bear and cub.

Hancock, Jesse E., Salem. Hermit crab, Salem Harbor.

Hatch, L., Salem. Sea robin.

Henderson, Daniel, Salem. Japanese tray brought home by Perry Exploring Expedition.

Hill, Wm. M., Salem. Deformed lobster claw.

Hitchings, E. H., Boston. Native plants collected near Boston.

Hoddell, John H., Salem. Malformed lobster claw.

Hodgdon, Adrial H., Wenham, Mass. Indian implement from Wenham.

Howell, Jos., Willamette Slough, Oregon. Specimens of *Montia Howelii.*

Humphreys, A., Salem. Cake of compressed tea prepared for transportation from China.

Hunt, T. F., Salem. Chinese water colors.

Johnson, Abbott, Wenham, Mass. Indian celt, granite nodule.

Johnson, Miss Kate, No. Andover, Mass. Alpine plants collected by Sam'l Johnson in Switzerland in 1860.

Jones, Geo. W., Wenham, Mass. Indian implements.

Jones, Warren, Wenham, Mass. Indian implements.

Kemble, Dr. L. G., Salem. Squid from Salem Harbor.

Keyes, W. H., East Saugus, Mass. Indian implements and minerals.

Kikuchi, Prof., Dairoku, Japan. Japanese objects.

Killam, Amos F., Danvers, Mass. Box turtle from Reading.

Kimball, Joel, Beverly, Mass. Indian implements and pottery from Salem and Essex.

Kimball, Mrs. M. W., Wenham, Mass. Gall on *Acer dasycar-pum*.

King, Miss Harriet, Salem. Insect.

King, Capt. Henry F., Salem. Nut galls, line from Fiji Islands.

Kingsley, J. S., Malden, Mass. Invertebrates from Annisquam, Mass.

Knowlton, C. Everett, Hamilton, Mass. Nest and eggs of indigo bird and Indian club head from Hamilton.

Knowlton, Ira P., Hamilton, Mass. Insect from apple tree.

Kunze, Chas., Lawrence, Mass. Stuffed specimen of German magpie.

Lake, Otto, Topsfield, Mass. Indian implements.

Larcom, John, Beverly Farms, Mass. Large spider.

Lee, Frank H., Salem. Bird's nest.

Leonard, Wm., Salem. Insect and abnormal apple.

Lewis, C. N., Salem. Striped snake.

Lindsey, N. Allen, Marblehead. Plants from Marblehead.

Low, John C., Ipswich, Mass. Mineral.

Lunt, B. S., Beverly, Mass. Ancient button.

Mack, Dr. Wm., Salem. Fur dress from northern Russia.

Martin, Edward C., Salem. Albino flounder taken off Thatcher's Island.

May, Edw. L., Beverly Farms, Mass. Black snake and spider.

McDaniel, Rev. B. F., Salem. Minerals from Newbury, etc.

McGrane, Wm., Salem. Large moth.

Milberry, Jas. S., Salem. Indian skull (female), Summer St., Salem.

Millett, Geo. L., Salem. Model Kiak from Greenland.

Mooney, Frank T., Salem. Cuttle fish, snakes in alcohol.

Morris, Chas. S., Salem. Water scorpion.

Morse, Edward S., Salem. Japanese objects, six photographs of Zuni Indians.

Morse, John G., Salem. Two kites, one toy bow and box of Japanese candy.

Moulton, Jas. T., Lynn, Mass. Indian relics.

Nevins, W. S., Salem. Claydonia from Mt. Washington.

Newcomb, R. L., Salem. Birds from Essex County.

Nichols, Andrew, jr., Danvers, Mass. Limestone from Danvers.

Northend, W. D., Salem. Minerals from Danbury, N. C.

Ober, A. K., Beverly, Mass. Human skull from Beverly, clay objects from Mexico.

Paine, Miss Harriet E., Groveland, Mass. Essex County plants.

Paine, Mrs. J. C., Groveland, Mass. Cyprea from South Pacific.

Palmer, Dr. Charles, Ipswich, Mass. Bonaparte's gull and cast of Indian carving from Ipswich.

Parker, Mrs., Groveland, Mass. Water newt.

Peabody, Henry W., Salem. Dust from eruption at Krakatoa, from deck of bark Wm. H. Besse.

Peabody, Francis, Topsfield, Mass. Ancient knife.

Perkins, Ezra, Essex, Mass. Caoutchouc from tree in British Guiana.

Perley, Edwin P., Danvers, Mass. Indian implement.

Perkins, Charles A., Wakefield, Mass. Indian relics from Wakefield.

Peterson, Joseph N., Salem. Main lock from Salem Jail; specimen of red bat.

Phillips, S., jr., Marblehead. *Ornathogalum umbellatum.*

Plumer, Miss Mary N., Salem. Plants for collection.

Piland, Eugene, Norfolk, Va. Fragment of stone from Pompey's Pillar, Egypt.

Pitman, Frank H., Salem. Five skins of lemur, Imerina, Central Madagascar.

Pratt, John J., Wakefield, Mass. Polished serpentine from Lynnfield.

Price, Miss J. C., Salem. Braid of girl's hair from Maulmain, Burmah.

Richardson, E. F., Marblehead, Mass. Beetle.

Robinson, Mrs. John, Salem. Japanese cloth.

Robinson, Mary and Lucy, Salem. Indian implements, plants, minerals, insects, etc., from Essex County.

Rogers, Dr. G. O., Boston, Mass. Totem and halibut hook from Alaska.

Ropes, Mrs. Charles A., Salem. Spider from Saratoga Springs.

Ropes, Reuben W., Salem. Albino night heron from Salem.

Ruee, Henry, Salem. Portrait of Thos. Ruee (to East India Marine Society.)

Russell, Peter, Salem. Two butterflies.

Russell, Wm., Salem. Bird's nest made of twine.

Sargent, Prof. C. S., Brookline, Mass. Collection of tested specimens of woods from Essex County.

Sears, George B., Danvers, Mass. Unio from peat ditch in Danvers.

Sears, John H., Salem. Minerals, Indian relics, etc., from Essex County; cones and mammals from Maine.

Sears, Wallace, Salem. Dragon fly.

Seymour, Prof. A. B., Champaign, Illinois. Collection of micro-fungi from Illinois.

Shatswell, James, Salem. *Cermatia forceps.*

Shorey, John L., Lynn, Mass. Pond turtle weighing twenty five pounds and eggs of turtle.

Silsbee, Wm. D., Salem. Eggs of Purpura, Beverly Bar.

Simes, Mrs. John D., Salem. Larva of insect.

Simon, Francis, Salem. Malformed hen's egg.

Smith, C. V., Lynn, Mass. Mineral and specimen from " Dungeon rock."

Smith, Dalday, Marblehead, Mass. Stones, shells, etc., from shellheap.

Smith, Mrs. E. A., Jersey City, N. J. Beads from a Tuskarora Indian chief.

Snow, John, Salem. American silk worm moth from Beverly.

Solomon, A. Ryland U., West Freehold, N. J. Three specimens of marl from New Jersey.

South, Arthur A., Beverly, Mass. Mole cricket from Chebacco.

Staniford, George E., Salem. Photograph of jail and house, Salem.

Stanton, Bertie W., Wenham, Mass. Indian implements.

Stevens, George, Newport, R. I. Cast of stone carving.

Stickney, W. J., Salem. Plate turned from ash wood.

Stone, Arthur R., Salem. Conserve pot from Manila ; snake, mineral, golden salamander and moth from Salem.

Tadgell, Henry L., Salem. Insects from Salem.

Takanaka, Seika, Tokio, Japan. Seven private seals and Japanese account book.

Tileston, Amelia, Salem. Spider.

Tindley, Dexter, Salem. Stickleback.

Toppan, Charles, Salem. Specimen of Yucca.

Treadwell, J. R., Salem. Indian arrowpoint from Salem.

Upton, Mrs. William F., Peabody, Mass. Minerals from Naples.

Vickary, N., Lynn, Mass. Essex County birds and arrowpoints.

Walsh, John, Salem. Concretionary rock from gravel.

Waters, David, Salem. *Lobipes hyperborea.*

Waters, J. Linton, Salem. English sparrow's nest and eggs ; eggs of domestic pigeon.

Watson, Miss C. A., North Andover. Owl from Danvers.

Webb, Wm. G., Salem. Ferns from Madagascar.

Welch, Wm. L., Salem. Two conjoined barnacles from a bark from Africa ; " Youpon " tea from North Carolina ; insect.

Wertheimber, Louis, Boston, Mass. Family shrine, Japan ; Korean tobacco.

Whipple, George M., Salem. Mineral from Newbury ; Indian implements from Virginia.

Whipple, Prescott, Salem. Two young turtles ; insects.

Wiggin, Mrs. Andrew J., South Peabody. Abnormal potato.

Willcomb, Joseph, Ipswich, Mass. Collection of Indian implements.

Willcomb, O. Clifton, Ipswich, Mass. Indian relics from Ipswich.

Williams, James S., Salem. Money from Travancore, India.

Williams, John S., Salem. White perch from Chebacco.

Wonson, Everett L., Gloucester, Mass. Twelve Essex County fishes.

Wood, Rev. J. G., London, Eng. Compound nest of Baya bird.

Woodbury, Wm. G., Beverly, Mass. Fossil from Grand Banks.
Worcester, Samuel, Salem. Insects.
Wyman, Wm., Marblehead, Mass. Walking stick insect and
    Indian implements.
Yamada, Eneas. Antique carrying shrine from Japan.
Young, Aaron C., Salem. Hermit crab from Beverly Bridge.
Yu Kil Chun, Salem. Korean letter.

ACCESSIONS BY EXCHANGE OR PURCHASE.

Collection of Korean objects from Count Von Mollendorf. Japanese shrine ; Arraphahoe flute ; ethnological objects from New Guinea, etc. ; dried plants from Department of Agriculture.

ACCESSIONS TO THE LIBRARY.

1884.

AMERICAN.

Baltimore, Md. Johns Hopkins University. Circulars, Vol.
    3, 1883, Vol. 4, Nos. 34–35, 1884. 4 papers.
    Peabody Institute. 17th Annual Report, 1884.
Boston, Mass. Society of Nat. Hist. Proc., 24 parts. Memoirs, 3 parts. Constitution and by-laws.
    Science Observer. Vol. 4, Nos. 7–10.
Buffalo, N. Y. Society Nat. Hist. Bulletin, Vol. 4, No. 4,
    1883.
Byfield, Mass. Dumner Academy. Cat., 1883–4. Cat. of
    members, 1884.
Cambridge, Mass. Museum of Comparative Zoölogy. Bulletin,
    6 numbers. Memoirs, 3 numbers. Annual Report,
    1883–4.
    Peabody Mus. Archæology. 16–17 Annual Report.

Cincinnati, Ohio. Nat. Hist. Soc. 2 Papers.

Gloucester, Mass. Sawyer Free Library. Outline of History of Library.

Haverhill, Mass. Bradford Academy. In Memoriam, 1884. Pamphlet.

Indianapolis, Indiana. Geological Survey of Indiana. 12th Report.

Ithaca, N. Y. Cornell University. Register, 1883–4.

Kentucky. State Geol. Survey. 7 Publications.

Lawrence, Mass. Lawrence Free Library. 12th Annual Report.

Middletown, Conn. Wesleyan Univ. 12th Annual Report of Curator of Mus.

New York, N. Y. Amer. Monthly Microscopical Jour. Vol. 5, Nos. 1–11.

Amer. Mus. Nat. Hist. Bulletin, Vol. 1, No. 5. 15th Annual Report.

Linnæan Soc. Trans., Vol. 2, 1884.

Philadelphia, Penn. Acad. Nat. Science. Proc., Jan.–Dec.

American Naturalist. Vol. 18, Nos. 1–12.

Library Co. Bulletin, 1884–5.

Zoölogical Soc. 12th Annual Report.

Poughkeepsie, N. Y. Vassar Bros. Institute. Trans., 1883–4.

Salem, Mass. Amer. Assoc. Advancement of Science. Proc., 1883.

Essex Institute. Bulletin, Vol. 15, Nos. 1–9. Vol. 16, Nos. 1–6. Account of Plummer Hall; Priced Cat. of Publications; "Weeds," a paper by John H. Sears.

San Francisco, Cal. Cal. Academy. Bulletin, No. 1.

St Louis, Mo. Academy of Science. Trans., Vol. 4, No. 3, 1883.

Urbana, Ohio. Central Ohio Sci. Association. Proc., Vol. 1, Pt. 1.

Washington, D. C. Dept. Agric. 3rd Annual Report of Entomological Committee, 1880–2. Agr. grasses of United States.

Astronom. and Meteorolog. Observations, 1880.

Commissioner of Education. Report, 1882–3.

Dept. Interior. Bureau Education. 2–3, 1884.

U. S. Geol. Survey, No. 1, 1883.

U. S. Fish Commission. Report, 1881–2. Bulletin, Vol. 3, 1883.

Smithsonian Institution. Report, 1882. Powell Ethnology Report, 1880–1. Ethnol. Direction relative to Indian tribes of U. S., Powell.

Treasury Dept. Finance Report, 1883.

U. S. National Museum. Proc. 46 nos.

Miscellaneous.

The Bushberg Catalogue, from Publishers.

History of Essex County, from W. C. Endicott.

Geol. Map of Coal tracks of Ohio. Benj. Smith.

Periodic Laws. John A. R. Newland.

Wages and Tariffs. E. J. Donnell.

Course and growth of fibro-vascular bundles in Palms. J. C. Branner.

Official Catalogue of Foreign Exhibition in Boston, two editions, from E. S. Morse.

Anthropology. Otis T. Mason.

Brief Account of some public collections of American Archæology in U. S., H. Phillips, jr.

Fifth report of State Board of Health, Lunacy and Charity of Mass.

Report of causes of destruction of evergreen forests of northern New England and N. Y. Dr. A. S. Packard, jr., 1883.

Micrometry, History of, report of National Committee at Chicago.

FOREIGN.

AUSTRIA.

Prague. K. K. Sternwarte. 1883.

Vienna. K. K. Geologischen Reichsanstalt. Jahrbuch, Jan.–July 1–2–3, Kaiserliche Akademie der Wissenchaften. 8 nos.

BELGIUM.

Bruxelles. Academie Royal des Sciences des Lettres et des Beaux Arts de Belgique. Annales 27. 4 papers.

DENMARK.

Copenhagen. Soc. Royale des Antiquaires du Nord. Aarb. for Nord. Oldkyn. 3, 1883 ; 4, 1884.
L'Acad. Royale de Copenhagen. Bulletin 1883, No. 2. Memoirs, Vol. 9, Nos. 5–6

FRANCE.

Bordeaux. Acad. des Sci. Actes de l'Acad., 1878, 1880–1. 1 Publi.
Lyons. Soc. Imper. des. Scie. Bel. Let. et Arts. Memoirs 26, 1883–4.
Paris. Soc. d'Ethnographie. Memoirs, Tome 13, 1875.
Soc. Geologique de France. Bull. 10–48, 1–4.

GERMANY.

Wiesbaden. Nassauischen Verein fur Naturkunde. Jahrbucher, 1883.
Munster. West. Provin. Verein fur Wissenchaften und Kunst. 1883.
Munchen. Koniglich Bay. Akad. der Wissen. Bavaria. 10 Publications.
Marburg. Gesell. der Naturwissenschaftliche. Sitz. 1882–83.
Leipzig. Zinchen. on Enganzungen zu der Phygiographie der Braunkohle.
Naturforschende Gesellschaft. 1883.
Konigsburg. Physikalisch-okonomische Gesellschaft. 1883–84.
Emden. Naturforschenden Gesellschaft. Jahres, 1882–83.

Dresden. Kais. Leop. Car. deutsche Akad. der Naturforsch.
Nova Acta 44, 1883.

Naturwissenschaftliche Gesellschaft. 1883, July–Dec.
1884, Jan., June.

Naturforschende Gesellschaft. 1884.

Brun. Naturforschen. Verein. Verhandlungen 22, 1883.

Bremen. Naturwissenschaftliche Verein. Abhandlungen 8–2,
9–1.

Braunschweig. Archiv. der Anthropologie. Bd. 13, Nos. 1–3,
1884.

Bonn. Naturhistorischer Verein der Preussischen Rheinlande
und Westphalen. 1883–84.

Berlin. Koniglich Preussische Akademie der Wissenschaften.
47 parts.

Gesell. Naturforschende freunde. Sitz., 1883.

Entomoligischer Verein. 28–1, 1884.

GREAT BRITAIN.

London. Entomol. Soc. Trans. 1883.

Geological Soc. Quarterly Jour., Vol. 40, Nos. 157–160.
List of Soc., Nov., 1884.

Royal Geog. Soc. Proc., Vol. 4, No. 1, Vol. 6, Nos. 1–11.

Royal Society. Proc. 227–235. Trans., Vol. 174, pts. 2–3,
1883.

The Council, 1883.

Zoölogical Soc. Proc. 1883–4, 1884, No. 1. List of Fellows.

British Museum. Guide to Nat. Hist. specimens.

R. A. Peacock. Paper on Volcanoes with suppl.

Liverpool. Mayer Museum. 21st annual report. Catalogue.

Brighton and Sussex Nat. Hist. Soc. Annual report, 1883–84.

Belfast, Ireland. Nat. Field Club. Annual report, 1882–83.

Dublin, Ireland. Roy. Irish Acad. Proc., Vol. 2, Nos. 1–4–5.
Trans. Vol. 28, Nos. 14–16.

Royal Soc. Proc., Vol. 3, Nos. 6–7,Vol. 4, Nos. 1–4. Trans.,
Vol. 1, 20–25, Vol. 3, Nos. 1–3.

Edinburgh, Scotland. Royal Soc. Proc., 1881–82. Trans. Vol.
30, 2–3, Vol. 31, –1. List of members.

GREAT BRITAIN, COLONIES.

Montreal, Canada. Geol. Surv. of Canada. 3 Vols.
Canadian Record of Science. Vol. 1, No. 1.

Toronto, Canada. Entomol. Soc. Annual report, 1883.

London, Canada. Canadian Entomologist. Vol. 16, Nos. 2–11.

Toronto, Canada. Canadian Institute. Proc. Vol. 2, Nos. 1–3, 1884.

Calcutta, India. Geol. Surv. of India. Memoirs 9 Nos. Records 7 Nos. Memoirs 3 Nos.
Rajah Tourindro Mohun Tagore, 7 papers, gift of Gen. C. B. Norton.

Sydney, N. S. Wales. Royal Soc. Jour. and Proc. Vol. 16, 1882, Vol. 18, 1883. Report of Australian Mines, 1883.

Adelaide, So. Australia. Royal Soc. Trans., Vol. 6, 1882.

HOLLAND.

Harlem. Teyler Museum. Archives, Ser. 2, 1883.

ITALY.

Florence. Societa Entomol. Bulletino, 4, 1883 ; 1, 1884.

JAPAN.

Tokio. Univ. of Tokio. Memoirs, No. 9. Okadaira Shell Mounds at Hitachi.

MADAGASCAR.

Antananarivo. Antan. Annual and Madagascar Magazine. Vol. 7, 1883.

MEXICO.

Mexico. El Museo Nacional. Annales, Vol. 3, No. 6.

NORWAY.

Christiana. Kongelige Norske Universitet. 4 Publications.

Trondjem. Kongelige Noriske Videnskabers Selskabs. Skrifter, 1881.

P. A. S.

RUSSIA.

St. Petersburg. Soc. Ent. de Russie. Horae 17, 1882.
Jardin Imperiale de Botanique. Acta Horti Petro. Vol.
8, 1–2.
Moscow. Soc. Imperiale des Naturalists de Moscou. Bull.,
1882–3, 1–4.

SWEDEN.

Upsala. Kongelige Vetenskaps Societeten. Nova Acta, Vol.
12–1.
Stockholm. Entomologist Tidskrift. Bd. 4, Heft 1–4. Bd. 5,
Heft 1–4.

SWITZERLAND.

Basel. Naturforschende Gesellschaft. Verhandlungen, 8–2.
Auhang., 7.
Geneva. Institut. Nat. Genevois Switzer. Bull. 25, 1883.
Lausanne. Societe Vaudoise des Sciences Naturelles. Bull.,
19, No. 89.
St. Gallen. Naturwissenschaftliche Gesellschaft. 1881–2.

ACCESSIONS TO THE LIBRARY BY PURCHASE.

1884.

Illustrated Natural History, Rev. J. G. Wood. 3 vols.
Illustrated Natural History of Man, Rev. J. G. Wood. 2 vols.
Historical Sketch of Salem, Essex Institute.
New England Bird Life, Coues and Stearns. 2 vols.
Genera Plantarum, Bentham and Hooker. 3 vols.
Seoane's Neuman and Baretti's Spanish Dictionary. 1 vol.
Adler's German Dictionary. 1 vol.
Spier's & Surenne's French Dictionary. 1 vol.
Boston Directory, last edition. 1 vol.
Salem Directory, 1884. 1 vol.
Atlas Essex Co., Walker. 1 vol.

Geological Story Briefly Told, Dana.   1 vol.
Elements ot Geology, Le Conte.   1 vol.
Manual of Geology, Dana.   1 vol.
New Text Book of Geology, Dana.   1 vol.
A Text Book of Mineralogy, Dana.   1 vol.
Manual of Mineralogy and Lithology, Dana.   1 vol.
Text Book of Geology, Geikie.   1 vol.
Structural and Systematic Conchology, Tryon.   Illust'd.   1 vol.

THE NATIVE WOODS

OF

ESSEX COUNTY, MASSACHUSETTS.

AN ACCOUNT OF THE GENERAL DISTRIBUTIONS AND USES, THE DE-
TERMINATIONS OF THE SPECIFIC GRAVITY, PERCENTAGE OF ASH,
STRENGTH, FUEL VALUE, ETC., OF THE WOODS OF THE NA-
TIVE TREES OF ESSEX COUNTY, AS SHOWN BY TESTS
UPON SPECIMENS FURNISHED
BY THE
PEABODY ACADEMY OF SCIENCE.

Extracted from the Report on the Forests of North America by Prof.
Chas. S. Sargent, published in vol. IX of the Reports of the Tenth
Census of the U. S., with notice of the scope of the report, tables,
etc., prepared by John Robinson.

[Printed with reports of Peabody Academy of Science for 1884.]

PRINTED FOR THE ACADEMY.

SALEM, MASS.

1885.

THE NATIVE WOODS OF ESSEX COUNTY, MASSACHUSETTS.

The following paper has been prepared for the purpose of giving, in condensed form, the results of experiments made with the woods of the native forest trees of Essex County, Mass., as shown by the report on the forest trees of the United States by Prof. Charles S. Sargent, and printed as the ninth volume of the reports of the tenth census.

Taking advantage of the opportunity offered by the work of the Forestry Department of the Tenth Census for obtaining accurate information in relation to our native woods, rough logs of all the native species of trees of the county were obtained and forwarded to Prof. Sargent by the Peabody Academy of Science. From these logs suitable pieces were prepared and passed through all the tests made, the results of which are given in various portions of the general report in connection with tests of the woods of all the trees of the United States.

Besides the logs obtained for this purpose by Mr. John H. Sears of the Academy, the following persons contributed additional specimens :—

Mr. Henry Merrill of West Newbury, *Nyssa sylvatica* (Tupelo), two logs.

Mr. Samuel Whipple of Hamilton, *Fagus ferruginea* (Beech).

Agt. Great Pasture Co., Salem, *Celtis occidentalis* (Nettle Tree).

Mr. William Sutton of Salem, *Betula nigra* (Red Birch), from N. Andover.

Mr. Andrew Nichols of Danvers, *Robinia viscosa* (Clammy Locust) and *Rhus typhina* (Sumach).

Mr. Quint of Peabody, *Prunus serotina* (Black Cherry).

Mr. J. P. Wallace of Salem, *Betula papyrifera* (Paper Birch), from Townsend.

Mr. Solomon Kimball of Wenham, *Ostrya Virginica* (Hop Hornbeam).

Mr. John A. Sears of Danvers, Locust, Walnut, Beech, Black Oak, etc.

Mr. Edward S. Rayner of North Reading, White and Pitch Pines, White and Red Oaks, Hornbeam, Hemlock, Pig-nut Hickory, White Ash, etc.

In all seventy-five specimens of fifty-three different species were collected and forwarded to Prof. Sargent. These included ten specimens of six shrubby species, the figures for the tests of which will be found in a separate table. The specimens tested cover, with three or four exceptions, all the trees which grow naturally in the county, and for these few the average results are given of tests made upon specimens of the same species of trees from other localities. The only tree among these, however, of any importance, is the Sugar Maple for which New England specimens in sufficient number were obtained, although none were from within the limits of Essex County.

Before proceeding to the descriptions and tables it has been thought best to give a sketch of the scope of Prof. Sargent's report inasmuch as the work itself will not be generally accessible although it will doubtless be found in the larger libraries of the county and certainly at the Peabody Academy in Salem where all residents of the county are welcome to examine it.

GENERAL REVIEW OF THE WORK.

"The Forests of North America exclusive of Mexico," by Charles S. Sargent, Arnold Professor of Arboriculture in Harvard College. Volume IX of the Publications of the Tenth Census of the United States, Washington, 1884. One volume, quarto, 612 pages, 32 colored maps, and portfolio with sixteen additional maps.

The investigations, the results of which are given in this volume, were conducted under the direction of Prof. Charles S. Sargent as special agent, in charge, in connection with the work of the tenth census and published by the United States Department of the Interior. The work was begun in the latter part of 1879 and continued unremittingly till the summer of 1883. To obtain accurate details in relation to the different species of the forest trees, the density and other statistics connected with the distribution of the forests, it was necessary to have various portions of the territory traversed by reliable explorers, in addition to the returns received from an elaborate system of circulars which were distributed throughout the country. For this purpose the services of several botanists of recognized ability were secured to whom different portions of the country were allotted, Professor Sargent journeying himself, in company with the late Dr. George Engelmann, through the northwestern portion of the United States, California and Arizona, and afterwards in Texas and the South Atlantic states. From the explorations and the returns the maps accompanying the report were made up. Besides this and the closet labor required to digest the statistical portions of the work, the preparation of botanical descriptions and extensive bibliography of the species, a full set of the woods of the country were to be obtained for the purpose of being tested to ascertain their value for fuel and for mechanical purposes. To obtain specimens of each of the four hundred and twelve trees enumerated in the catalogue, was in many cases very difficult, yet they were all finally secured with the exception of seven species, trees either of very limited range or only known from the reports of early explorers, none of which possess any commercial value.

Of the more important trees many specimens were obtained from widely different regions of their distribution.

The specimens thus collected were properly dried and made up into sticks and blocks of the required length and shape for testing in various ways. The specific gravity and ash determinations were made by Mr. S. P. Sharples of Cambridge, and the tests for strength were made upon the United States testing machine at the Watertown arsenal. In addition to the assistance of our own botanists, Professor Sargent was also indebted to the members of the Canadian Geological Survey for valuable assistance in relation to the northern forests.

Heretofore works upon this subject have only given in a very general way the results of investigations of forest trees of a region. This is the first instance where the scientific name of each tree has been carefully connected with the specimen tested, and where all specimens have been tested under precisely the same conditions, and, where for strength tests, pieces of exactly the same size have been used throughout for the experiments. The text of the report is illustrated by thirty-nine colored maps with sixteen larger ones in a separate portfolio showing the distribution of all the important trees, the relative density of the forests, the nature of the fuel used throughout the country, etc.

The report is divided into three parts: Part I is devoted to the catalogue of species with remarks upon their synonymy, bibliography, distribution, uses, etc. ; Part II to the woods, their specific gravity, strength, comparative values, etc., and Part III to the economic aspects of the forests.

The catalogue with its copious index occupies some two hundred and twenty pages and enumerates four hundred and twelve species which include such varieties as are considered worthy of recognition. "To keep the catalogue within reasonable limits" the line between trees and shrubs, an arbitrary distinction, is settled by admitting as trees those "species which grow from the ground with a single stem either wholly or over a large portion of their distribution." Much labor has been expended upon the bibliography of the species, in many instances upwards of one hundred, and in one case one hundred and twenty-five, references being cited, exclusive of separate editions of the same work. Investigations of the work of earlier botanical writers has led to changes in the names of several of our common trees, thus, the Southern Pine usually known as *Pinus australis*, Mx. f., becomes *P. palustris*, Miller; the northern Tupelo known as *Nyssa multiflora*, Wang., has been united with several southern forms as one species under *N. sylvatica*, Marshall; the Hornbeam, formerly *Carpinus Americana*, Lamark, becomes *C. Caroliniana*, Walter; and the Northern Hemlock is changed from *Abies* to *Tsuga Canadensis*, Carriere. These changes are based upon the priority of the date of the description of the species. Part I of this work will be of the greatest value to the botanists as regards synonymy, distribution of the species and the bibliography, while the terse descriptions of the nature of the wood taken in connection with the distribution of the species furnishes important data for the builder and mechanic.

The object of the experiments, the results of which are given in detail for each specimen of every species in several extended tables in Part II, was to determine, "first, the fuel value of the woods of the United States, and second, the value of the wood of the principal trees of the country as material for construction;" the last results being obtained by experiments made with the United States testing machine at the Watertown arsenal.

The fuel value of the woods was reached by "a determination of the specific gravity and ash of the absolutely dry woods supplemented by a determinaiion of the actual chemical composition of the woods of some of the most important trees." In these experiments, except in rare instances, "at least two determinations were made for each species studied and, in the case of woods of commercial importance, specimens were taken from many trees growing in widely different parts of the country and under different conditions of soil and climate."

The figures indicating the specific gravity of all the woods of the United States fall between that of *Condalia ferrea*, a semi-tropical tree of southern Florida, 1.3020, and that of *Ficus aurea*, a species of fig, 0.2616. Arranged in the order of their weights, the first sixty-three specimens include but one North Atlantic tree, the unimportant *Cratœgus coccinea* (Scarlet Thorn), the majority coming from southern Florida or the southwest, the first sixteen species being heavier than water. Among the important North Atlantic species *Carya alba* (Shagbark Hickory) stands first at .8372 closely followed by *Quercus obtusiloba* (Post Oak) and *Ostrya Virginica* (Hop Hornbeam). *Sequoia gigantea* (Giant Red Wood) is the lightest wood of any account (0.2882), the eastern Arbor Vitæ and White Cedar being but slightly heavier.

"All species in which the wood is heavier than water belong to the semi-tropical region of Florida or to the arid Mexican and interior Pacific region." There exists "a relation between aridity of climate and the weight of the wood," even in single species of wide distribution. *Quercus prinoides* from Texas is nineteen per cent heavier than the average of all other specimens of the same species from other parts of the country, and the wood of the southern variety of White Ash is twenty per cent heavier than the average of all the northern specimens; variations in other species might be cited in illustration although there are occasional exceptions to the rule. For all the species "the relative fuel values" of the woods were "obtained by deducting the percentage of ash from the specific gravity," but, in the case of nearly all the important trees analyses were made "and their absolute fuel value calculated." The experiments show that equal weights of resinous woods give upwards of twelve per cent more heat than non-resinous woods. Making this allowance, the theory advanced by Count Rumford that equal weights of woods possess the same fuel value without regard to specific distinction, stands substantially correct, and the specific gravity tests give a direct means for comparison for heat values. In burning wood other factors are to be considered; fireplaces are not constructed to fully utilize the fuel value of resinous woods and the amount of water contained in woods greatly affects the result. In the table of actual values, seventy tests are given of sixty-three important species. Of the resinous woods, considered by volume, the southern Pine stands first; by weight, however, the North Atlantic Pitch Pine leads it, although standing as the sixth species when considered by volume. These are closely followed by the Port Orford Cedar of Oregon, and the South Atlantic Pond Pine. Of the non-resinous woods, considered by volume, the *Cercocarpus* of the interior Pacific region leads, followed by the Hickories and the *Oriodoxa* (Royal

Palm) of Florida, yet by weight the *Oriodoxa* leads, followed by the *Mesquit* and the black variety of the Rock Maple.

In the experiments to ascertain resistance to transverse pressure the sticks used were made four centimeters square and placed on bearings exactly one meter apart, pressure being applied to the centre. For longitudinal compression the blocks were four centimeters square and sixteen centimeters long. Transverse resistance tests of several species were also made with pieces eight centimeters square. Tests of all species were made to ascertain the resistance to pressure applied perpendicularly to the fibres, and others to ascertain the elasticity of the woods. For transverse strength the Nutmeg Hickory leads, followed in order by the *Amyris sylvatica*, of Florida, *Robinia Pseudacacia* (Locust) and *Quercus chrysolepis* (Live Oak) of the Pacific. The tests for transverse strength also show that such strength closely follows the specific gravity of the specimens. For longitudinal strength the heavy tropical woods of Florida stand at the head, and for elasticity the *Larix occidentalis* (Larch) of the Pacific coast comes first, while the Lignum Vitæ from the Florida Keys best resists indentation.

Determinations were made of the amount of tannin in the bark of twenty-three different species, and although the results do not indicate the actual values of the bark for tanning purposes, other matters entering into consideration in practice, yet these tests will indicate species, not now in use, "which may be looked to as possible sources for tannin supplies." Of these the *Rhizophora Mangle* of southern Florida shows 31.05 per cent. of tannin, *Gordonia Lasianthus* of the Southern States 13.14, *Picea Engelmanni* 12.60 to 20.56 and the Douglas Fir 12.79 per cent.

The tables above quoted cover some two hundred and forty pages and furnish a great amount of interesting and valuable information, but the results of the experiments which they record "must not, however, be considered as conclusive, but rather valuable, as indicating what lines of research should be followed in a more thorough study of the subject." As large a number of specimens were tested as it was possible to obtain of each species and enough of all important species to avoid errors arising from insufficient material, yet, for want of uniformity in the wood of a single species, further tests would quite likely cause a sufficient variation of the result to change the relative position held by that species, especially as so large a number of determinations fall between such narrow limits. While, therefore, the position among any ten or even twenty numbers may be considered as accidental, yet the tests furnish very satisfactory general results. Thus, for transverse strength, the Locust, Hickories and Oaks surpass the Maples, Ashes and Elms; and for resistance to crushing pressure, tropical species surpass the northern ones, and we may ascertain, too, from what situation and soil the strongest growth is obtained and which species of a genus are best adapted to our needs.

In summing up the results of the experiments Prof. Sargent says : "The various tests made upon the woods of North America indicate at least the important fact that, within the limits of any species, the weight and strength of any specimen of wood depend upon the actual proportion of the space occupied in the layers of the annual growth, with open ducts to the space occupied with compact, woody tissue, and to the size of these ducts; or in the case of the wood of Coniferæ, the proportion of space occupied with cells formed early in the season to that occupied with smaller cells of the summer growth. The causes which thus affect the growth of the wood are not very apparent. It is not soil, nor age, nor general climatic conditions, ... nor does the rapidity of growth, as has been supposed, greatly affect the strength of wood, because the proportion of open to compact growth is little affected by rapid or slow increase of the tree's diameter."

"It follows that while such experiments are necessary to establish maximum and relative values for any species, these being established, actual values of any given specimen of wood may be determined by microscopic examination of its structure ; that is, two specimens of the wood of any species to which the census tests have been applied being given, their relative values can be determined by an examination of their structure as well as, or better than by any elaborate experiments."

Passing to Part III, the "economic aspects" of the forests are considered. Here it is shown that our forests furnish the larger portion of our citizens with fuel and the material for much of the mechanical construction. No country in the world was ever more liberally supplied with timber-producing trees, either as regards quantity, quality or variety, than our own, and yet these gifts have been shamefully misused. With the axe we have ruthlessly cut down ten trees where we have. used one, and by allowing fire to seize upon the cut over woodlands and spread into the uncut, hundreds of trees have been destroyed where ten have been cut. The facts are here presented which must be the basis of our dealings with a question of national importance. In the census year (1880) the estimated value of the forest crop, including every article that can possibly be utilized, was seven hundred millions of dollars. Of this amount nearly one-half was known to be used as fuel. Fire destroyed trees, at the standing value to the amount of twenty-five and one-half million dollars. But this destruction of trees by fire is trifling compared to the injury done to the land which was burned over, for not only are the old and young trees destroyed, together with the seeds lying in the soil ready in the course of nature to germinate, but the soil itself is rendered unfit for immediate forest production. Generations of other plants must first flourish and decay before there will again be a forest of commercial value upon it, for this land cannot produce a marketable forest for one hundred years. It is gratifying, however, to learn that the forests of Maine are now realized to be of such vital importance that protection from fire and over-cutting has been rendered possible. This is pointed out in the report as the one hopeful example in the whole country.

The forests of each of the different states are treated separately, those of Massachusetts, however, being considered in connection with Connecticut and Rhode Island. Of this section the report says : — "The original forests which covered these states have disappeared" and have in some cases been replaced by even a fourth growth of trees. "The area covered by tree growth in these states is slowly increasing, although with the exception of the forests of young White Pine, the productive capacity of their woodlands . . . is rapidly diminishing." Abandoned farming land, if protected from fire and browsing animals, except in the immediate vicinity of the coast, is soon very generally covered with a vigorous growth of White Pine. This promises to give more than local importance to these forests in the future. "In Massachusetts during the year 1880, 13,899 acres of woodland were reported as destroyed by fire, with a loss of upwards of one hundred and two thousand dollars. Of these fires fifty-two were set by locomotives, forty-five were started on farms and escaped to forests, thirty-seven were caused by hunters, nineteen by the careless use of tobacco, eight through malice and three by carelessness in the manufacture of charcoal." The principal forests of Massachusetts are in Berkshire, Hampden and Worcester Counties.

"In Barnstable County numerous experiments in forest planting have been made. In South Orleans and the neighboring towns fully 10,000 acres of sandy, barren soil have been successfully and profitably planted with Pitch Pine," and there are other plantations in Plymouth, Bristol and Nantucket.

In conclusion Prof. Sargent says : — "The forest wealth of the country is still undoubtedly enormous ; yet it is by no means inexhaustible, for, in spite of their great extent, variety and richness, and the fact that the climatic conditions of a large portion of the country are peculiarly favorable to the development of a forest growth, they cannot always be productive if the simplest laws of nature governing their growth are disregarded."

DESCRIPTION AND USES OF THE WOOD AND DISTRIBUTION OF THE NATIVE TREES OF ESSEX COUNTY; EXTRACTED FROM THE FORESTRY REPORT.

THE numbers of the species in the following list are those of Prof. Sargent's catalogue of all the trees of North America north of Mexico. This list includes several species of trees which are only shrubs in Essex County and it does not include certain shrubs which, although of larger growth here than some of those which are included, do not, however, in any portion of their distribution, become trees. With the exception of a few sentences giving the local distribution of the species, all the matter is taken directly from the forestry report; therefore, no quotation marks are used. As this paper deals only with the woods, all botanical descriptions of the trees are omitted, but such may be found, however, in "Gray's Manual of Botany" or in "Emerson's Trees and Shrubs of Massachusetts."

2. *Magnolia glauca,* Linnæus. Magnolia, Sweet Bay.

Distribution: Cape Ann, Mass.; New Jersey to Texas; swamps in Gloucester and Essex. A tree 15 to 22 meters in height, with a trunk sometimes 1.20 meters in diameter, or towards its northern limits reduced to a low shrub. Wood light, soft, not strong, close-grained, compact; medullary rays very numerous, thin; color, light brown tinged with red, the sap wood nearly white; in the Gulf States sometimes used in the manufacture of broom handles and small wooden ware.

17. *Tilia Americana,* Linnæus. Bass Wood, American Linden.

Distribution: northern New Brunswick to Texas; common in Essex County. Wood light, soft, not strong, very close-grained, compact, easily worked; color, light brown or often tinged with slight red, the sap wood hardly distinguishable; largely used in the manufacture of wooden ware and cheap furniture, for the panels and bodies of carriages, the inner soles of shoes, in turnery, and the manufacture of paper pulp (the quickly discolored sap renders it unfit for making white paper). The inner bark macerated is sometimes manufactured into coarse cordage and matting; the flowers, rich in honey, are highly prized by apiarists.

22. *Xanthoxylum Americanum*, Miller. Prickly Ash.

Distribution: eastern Mass. to northern Missouri; Danvers to Georgetown, etc. A shrub in Essex County. A small tree; wood light, soft, coarse grained; color, light brown, the sap wood lighter; the bark of Xanthoxylum, an active stimulant, is used in decoction to produce diaphoresis in cases of rheumatism, syphilis, etc., and a popular remedy for toothache (U. S. Dispensatory, etc.).

58. *Acer Pennsylvanicum*, Linnæus. Striped Maple.

Distribution: valley of the St. Lawrence river, northern Atlantic states to northern Georgia, west to northern Minnesota; cool woods in Essex County. Wood light, soft, close grained, compact, satiny; color, light brown, the sap wood lighter.

64. *Acer saccharinum*, Wangenheim. Sugar Maple. Rock Maple.

Distribution: southern Newfoundland, west to Minnesota, and south to eastern Texas; common in Essex County. Wood heavy, hard, strong, tough, close-grained, compact, susceptible of a good polish; color, light brown, tinged with red, the sap-wood lighter, largely used in the manufacture of furniture, shoe lasts and pegs, saddle-trees, in turnery, for interior finish and flooring: in ship-building for keels, keelsons, shoes, etc., and furnishing valuable fuel; "curled maple" and "bird's eye" maple, accidental forms in which the grain is beautifully curled and contorted, are common and highly prized in cabinet making. Maple sugar is principally made from this species; the ashes of the wood, rich in alkali, yield large quantities of potash.

65. *Acer dasycarpum*, Ehrhart. White Maple.

Distribution: New Brunswick, south to western Florida west to Kansas and the Indian territory; Ipswich river, etc., in Essex county. Wood light, hard, strong, brittle, close-grained, compact, easily worked; somewhat used in the manufacture of cheap furniture, for flooring, etc.; maple sugar is occasionally made from this species.

66. *Acer rubrum*, Linnæus. Red Maple.

Distribution: New Brunswick south to Florida west to Indian territory and Texas; common in Essex County. Wood heavy, hard, not strong, close-grained, compact, easily worked; color, brown, often tinged with red, the sapwood lighter; largely used in cabinet making, turnery, and for wooden ware, gun stocks, etc.; an accidental variety with undulating grain is highly valued. Ink is occasionally made, domestically, by boiling the bark of this species in soft water and combining the tannin with sulphate of iron; formerly somewhat used in dyeing.

70. *Rhus typhina*, Linnæus. Staghorn Sumach.

Distribution: New Brunswick to Mississippi; common in Essex County. A small tree; wood light, brittle, soft, coarse-grained, compact, satiny, susceptible of a good polish; color, yellow streaked with green, the sapwood nearly white; occasionally used for inlaying cabinet work; the young shoots for "sap quills" in drawing the sap out of the sugar maple. Bark and leaves stringent, rich in tannin, and somewhat used locally as a dye in dressing skins; an infusion of the berries used domestically as a gargle in cases of catarrhal sore throat.

72. *Rhus venenata*, De Candolle. Poison Sumach.

Distribution: northern New England south to Louisiana west to Arkansas; swamps, common in Essex County. Wood light, soft, coarse-grained, moderately compact; color, light yellow streaked with brown, the sap-wood lighter; the whole plant, as well as the allied *R. Toxicodendron*, to most persons exceedingly poisonous to the touch, owing to the presence of a volatile principle, toxicodrendric acid; the white, milky sap turning black in drying and yielding a valuable lacquer.

77. *Robinia Pseudacacia*, Linnæus. Locust.

Distribution: Alleghany mountains, Pennsylvania to northern Georgia; widely and generally naturalized throughout the United States, east of the Rocky mountains; found throughout Essex County. Wood heavy, exceedingly hard and strong, close-grained, compact, very durable in contact with the ground; color, brown or, more rarely, light green, the sap-wood yellow; largely used in ship building, for posts of all sorts, construction, and in turnery; preferred to other American woods for treenails, and in this form largely exported. The bark of the root tonic, or in large doses purgative and emetic; formerly widely planted as a timber tree; its cultivation in the United States now generally abandoned on account of the destructive attacks of the locust borer.

78. *Robinia viscosa*, Ventenat. Clammy Locust.

Distribution: Alleghany mountains to North Carolina; widely cultivated and now occasionally naturalized in the Atlantic States; common in cultivation in Essex County. Wood (of a cultivated specimen) heavy, hard, close-grained, compact; color, brown, the sap-wood light yellow.

105. *Prunus Pennsylvanica*, Linnæus f. Wild Red Cherry.

Distribution : Labrador to Pennsylvania, North Carolina and Tennessee, and to the Rocky mountains of Colorado ; common in cleared lands in Essex County. Wood light, soft, close-grained, compact; color, light brown, sap-wood clear yellow ; the small acid fruit used domestically and by herbalists in the preparation of cough mixtures, etc.

108. *Prunus serotina*, Ehrhart. Wild Black Cherry.

Distribution : southern Ontario to Florida, west to Dakota and Texas ; common by walls and roadsides in Essex County. Wood light, hard, strong, close, straight-grained, compact; color, light brown or red, growing darker with exposure, the thin sap-wood yellow ; largely used and esteemed in cabinet work, interior finish, etc., and now becoming scarce. The bark contains a bitter tonic principle, employed as a tonic and sedative in cases of pulmonary consumption ; the bitter fruit used domestically in the preparation of cherry brandy.

127–8–9. *Cratægus coccinea*, Linnæus, Scarlet Thorn ; *C. subvillosa*, Schrader, Scarlet Haw and *C. tomentosa*, Linnæus, Black Thorn.

Closely allied species found in Essex County as shrubs ; 128 in Ipswich (Oakes about 1840). Wood heavy, hard, not strong; color, reddish brown.

137. *Amelanchier Canadensis*, Torrey and Gray. June Berry Shad Bush.

Distribution : Newfoundland to Florida and Indian territory ; common in Essex County. Wood heavy, exceedingly hard, close-grained, checking somewhat in seasoning, satiny, susceptible of a good polish ; color, dark brown, often tinged with red, the sap-wood much lighter.

138. *Hamamelis Virginica*, Linnæus. Witch Hazel.

Distribution: northern New England to Texas. common in Essex County. Wood heavy, hard, very close-grained, compact; layers of annual growth hardly distinguishable; color, light brown, tinged with red, the sap-wood nearly white; the bark and leaves rich in tannin, used in the form of fluid extracts, decoctions, etc., in external applications and as a reputed remedy in hemorrhoidal affections.

150. *Cornus alternifolia*, Linnæus f. Dogwood.

Distribution: New Brunswick west to Lake Superior, south to Alabama; common in Essex County. Wood heavy, hard, close-grained, checking badly in drying; color, brown tinged with red, the sap-wood light yellow.

151. *Cornus florida*, Linnæus. Flowering Dogwood.

Distribution: southern New England, Minnesota and through the Atlantic forests to Florida and Texas; found as a shrub in Gloucester, Wenham Swamp, Boxford, etc., in Essex County; rather scarce. Wood heavy, hard, close-grained, strong, tough, checking badly in drying, satiny, susceptible of a beautiful polish; color, brown, changing in different specimens to shades of green and red, the sap-wood lighter; used in turnery, for wood engravings, and the bearings of machinery, hubs of wheels, barrel hoops, etc. The bark, especially of the root, in common with that of other species of the genus, possesses bitter tonic properties, and is used in decoctions, in intermittent and malarial fevers.

154. *Nyssa sylvatica*,* Marshall (*N. multiflora*, Wang.) Tupelo.

Distribution: valley of the Kennebec river, Maine to Florida and Texas; frequent in low grounds in Essex

---

* Various forms of Nyssa in the Forestry Report are united into one polymorphous species, which may properly bear Marshall's earlier name of *Nyssa sylvatica*.

County. Wood heavy, rather soft, strong, very tough, unwedgeable, difficult to work, inclined to check unless carefully seasoned, not durable in contact with the soil, color, light yellow often nearly white, the sap-wood hardly distinguishable; now largely used for hubs of wheels, rollers in glass factories, ox yokes, and on the gulf coast for wharf piles.

158. *Viburnum Lentago*, Linnæus. Sheepberry.

Distribution: southern shores of Hudson bay to Missouri and along the Alleghany mountains to Georgia; common as a shrub in Essex County. Wood heavy, hard, close-grained, compact, emitting a disagreeable odor; color, dark orange-brown, the sap-wood nearly white.

170. *Kalmia latifolia*, Linnæus. Laurel.

Distribution: New Brunswick to Florida and Louisiana; a shrub in Essex County, frequent in the northern portion and on Cape Ann. Wood heavy, hard, strong, brittle, close-grained, compact; color, brown tinged with red, the sap-wood somewhat lighter; used for tool handles, in turnery, and for fuel. The leaves, buds and fruit, reputed poisonous to cattle, are occasionally used medicinally.

192. *Fraxinus Americana*, Linnæus. White Ash.

Distribution: Nova Scotia to Florida, west to Indian Territory and Texas; common in Essex County. Wood heavy, hard, strong, ultimately brittle, coarse-grained, compact; color, brown, sap-wood much lighter, often nearly white; largely used in the manufacture of agricultural implements, carriages, handles, oars, and for interior and cabinet work.

193. *Fraxinus pubescens*, Lamarck. Red Ash.

Distribution: New Brunswick to Florida, and Alabama; Ipswich river, etc., not very common in Essex County.

Wood heavy, hard, strong, brittle, coarse-grained, compact; color, rich brown, the sap-wood light brown streaked
with yellow; somewhat used as a substitute for the more
valuable white ash, with which it is often confounded.

198. *Fraxinus sambucifolia*, Lamarck. Black Ash.

Distribution: southern Newfoundland to shores of
Lake Winnipeg, south to Delaware and Arkansas; low
lands, occasional, in Essex County. Wood heavy, soft,
not strong, tough, rather coarse-grained, compact, durable, separating easily into thin layers; color, dark brown,
the sap-wood light brown, or often nearly white; largely
used for interior finish, fencing, barrel hoops, in cabinet
making, and the manufacture of baskets.

217. *Sassafras officinale*, Nees. Sassafras.

Distribution. Eastern Massachusetts to Iowa and south
to Florida and Texas; frequent in Essex County. Wood
light, soft, not strong, brittle, coarse-grained, very durable in contact with the soil, slightly aromatic, checking
in drying; color, dull orange-brown, the thin sap-wood
light yellow; used for light skiffs, ox yokes, etc., and
largely used for fence posts, rails and in cooperage. The
root, especially its bark, is a powerful aromatic stimulant;
the oil of sassafras, distilled from the root, is largely used
in imparting a pleasant flavor to many articles of domestic
use; the pith of the young branches infused with water
furnishes a mucilage used as demulcent in febrile and
inflammatory affections. "Gumbo filet," a powder prepared by the Choctaw Indians of Louisiana from the
mucilaginous leaves, is used at the south in the preparation of "Gumbo" soup.

225. *Ulmus fulva*, Michaux. Slippery Elm.

Distribution: valley of the lower Saint Lawrence to
Florida and Texas; Boxford, etc.; scarce in Essex County.
Wood heavy, hard, strong, very close-grained, compact,

durable, in contact with the ground, splitting readily when green ; color, dark brown or red, the thin sap-wood lighter ; largely used for wheel stock, fence posts, rails, railway ties, sills, etc. The inner bark mucilaginous, nutritious, and extensively used in various medicinal preparations.

224. *Ulmus Americana*, Linnæus. American Elm.

Distribution : southern Newfoundland to Rocky mountains, south to Florida ; common in Essex County. Wood heavy, hard, strong, tough, rather coarse-grained, compact, difficult to split ; color, light brown, the sap-wood somewhat lighter, largely used for wheel stock, saddle-trees, flooring, in cooperage, and now largely exported to Great Britain and used in boat and ship-building.

228. *Celtis occidentalis*, Linnæus. Hackberry. Nettle Tree.

Distribution : valley of the Saint Lawrence river to Dakota, south to Florida and Texas ; Salem, Plum Island, Boxford, etc. ; scarce in Essex County. Varying greatly in size, shape, and texture of the leaves, the extreme forms united make one polymorphous species of wide geographical range. Wood heavy, rather soft, not strong, coarse-grained, compact, satiny, susceptible of a good polish ; color, clear light yellow, the sap-wood lighter ; largely used for fencing and occasionally in the manufacture of cheap furniture.

235. *Platanus occidentalis*, Linnæus. Button Wood.

Distribution : southern Maine west to Kansas, south to Florida, and Texas ; scattered in Essex County. The largest tree of the Atlantic forests, often 30 to 40 meters in height, with a trunk 2.40 to 4.20 meters in diameter ; generally along streams and river bottoms. Wood heavy, hard, not strong, very close-grained, compact, difficult to split and work ; color, brown tinged with red, the sapwood lighter ; largely used for tobacco boxes (its principal use), ox yokes, butcher's blocks, and, rarely, in the manufacture of cheap furniture.

238. *Juglans cinerea*, Linnæus. Butternut.

Distribution: southern New Brunswick to Minnesota, south to Alabama; common in Essex County. Wood light, soft, not strong, rather coarse-grained, compact, easily worked, satiny, susceptible of a beautiful polish; color, bright light brown, turning dark with exposure, the sap-wood lighter; largely used for interior finish, cabinet work, etc.

242. *Carya alba*, Nuttall. Shag-bark Hickory.

Distribution: valley of the Saint Lawrence to Minnesota, south to Kansas and Texas; common in Essex County. A large tree of the first economic value, reaching its greatest development west of the Alleghany mountains. Wood heavy, very hard and strong, tough, close-grained, compact, flexible; color, brown, the thin and more valuable sap-wood nearly white; largely used in the manufacture of agricultural implements, carriages, ax handles, baskets, etc. The sweet and edible nuts afford an important article of commerce. The heaviest Essex County wood.

245. *Carya porcina*, Nuttall. Pig Nut.

Distribution: southern Maine to Minnesota, south to Florida and Texas; common in Essex County. Wood heavy, hard, very strong and tough, flexible, close-grained, checking in drying; color, dark or light brown, the thick sap-wood lighter, often nearly white; used for the same purposes as the shell-bark (shag-bark) hickory.

246. *Carys amara*, Nuttall. Bitter Nut.

Distribution: southern Maine to Kansas and Indian territory, south to Florida and Texas; frequent in Essex County. Wood heavy, very hard, strong, tough, close-grained, checking in drying; color, dark brown, the thick sap-wood light brown, or often nearly white ; largely used for hoops, ox yokes, etc.

249. *Myrica cerifera*, Linnæus. Bayberry.

Distribution : shores of Lake Erie, south to Florida and Alabama ; a very common shrub in Essex County. A tree sometimes 12 meters in height, with a trunk 0.30 to 0.45 meters in diameter, reaching its greatest development in the bottoms and rich hummocks of the Georgia and Florida coasts. Wood light, soft, strong, brittle, very close-grained, compact ; color, dark brown, the sapwood lighter ; the leaves and stimulant and astringent bark of the roots sometimes employed by herbalists. The wax which covers the small globular fruit, formerly largely collected and made into candles, and now, under the name of myrtle-wax, a popular remedy in the treatment of dysentery.

251. *Quercus alba*, Linnæus. White Oak.

Distribution : northern Maine to Florida and Texas ; common in Essex County ; the large trees are fast disappearing. Wood strong, very heavy, hard, tough, close-grained, liable to check unless carefully seasoned, durable in contact with the soil ; color, brown, the sap-wood lighter brown ; largely used in ship-building, construction of all sorts, cooperage, in the manufacture of carriages, agricultural implements, and baskets, and for railway ties, fencing, interior finish, cabinet-making, fuel, etc. A decoction of the astringent inner bark is employed in cases of hemorrhage, dysentery, etc.

258. *Quercus bicolor*, Willdenow. Swamp White Oak.

Distribution : southern Maine to Missouri and south to Kentucky and Arkansas ; common in low lands in Essex County. Wood heavy, hard, strong, tough, close-grained, inclined to check in seasoning ; color, light brown, the sap-wood hardly distinguishable; used for the same purposes as that of the white oak.

261. *Quercus prinoides*, Willdenow. Chinquapin Oak.

Distribution: eastern Massachusetts to Kansas south to Mississippi and Texas; Peabody, Topsfield, Boxford, etc., a shrub in Essex County. A tree 24 to 30 meters in height (*Q. Muhlenbergii*), or often, reduced to a low, slender shrub (*Q. prinoides*). Wood heavy, hard, very strong, close-grained, checking badly in drying, very durable in contact with the soil; color, dark brown, the sap-wood much lighter; used for cooperage, wheel stock, fencing, railway ties, etc. The small acorns sweet and edible.

272. *Quercus rubra*, Linnæus. Red Oak.

Distribution: Nova Scotia to Kansas, south to Florida and Texas; common in Essex County. Wood heavy hard, strong, close-grained, inclined to check in drying; color, light brown or red, the sap-wood somewhat darker; now largely used for clapboards, cooperage and somewhat for interior finish, in the manufacture of chairs, etc.

273. *Quercus coccinea*, Wangenheim. Scarlet Oak.

Distribution: southern Maine to Missouri, south to Florida; occasional in Essex County. Wood heavy, hard, strong, coarse-grained, color, light brown or red, the sap-wood rather darker; if used at all, confounded with that of *Q. rubra*.

274. *Quercus tinctoria*, Bartram. Black Oak.

Distribution: southern Maine to Florida and Texas; common in Essex County. Wood heavy, hard, strong, not tough, coarse-grained, liable to check in drying; color, bright brown tinged with red, the sap-wood much lighter; somewhat used for cooperage, construction, etc. The bark largely used in tanning: the intensely bitter inner bark yields a valuable yellow dye, and is occasionally used medicinally.

290. *Castanea vulgaris*, var. *Americana*, A. DeCandolle. Chestnut.

Distribution: southern Maine to Michigan, south to Alabama and Tennessee; not very common in Essex County. Wood light, soft, not strong, coarse-grained, liable to check and warp in drying, easily split, very durable in contact with the soil; color, brown, the sapwood lighter; largely used in cabinet-making, for railway ties, posts, fencing, etc. The fruit, although smaller, superior in sweetness and flavor to that of the European chestnut. An infusion or fluid extract of the dried leaves is successfully employed in the treatment of whooping-cough and other pectoral affections.

291. *Fagus ferruginea*, Aiton. Beech.

Distribution: Nova Scotia to Wisconsin, south to Florida and Texas; frequent in Essex County. Wood very hard, strong, tough, very close-grained, not durable in contact with the soil, inclined to check in drying, difficult to season, susceptible of a beautiful polish; color, varying greatly with soil and situation, dark red, or often lighter, the sap-wood nearly white; largely used in the manufacture of chairs, shoe-lasts, plane-stocks, handles, etc., and for fuel.

292. *Ostrya Virginica*, Willdenow. Hop Hornbeam.

Distribution: Bay of Chaleur to Minnesota, south to Florida and Texas; frequent in Essex County. Wood heavy, very strong and hard, tough, very close-grained, compact, susceptible of a beautiful polish, very durable in contact with the soil; color, light brown tinged with red, or, like the sap-wood, often nearly white; used for posts, levers, handles of tools, etc.

293. *Carpinus Caroliana*, Walter. (*C. Americana*, Lam.) Hornbeam.

Distribution: Nova Scotia to Minnesota, south to Florida and Texas; frequent in Essex County. Wood heavy, very strong and hard, close-grained, inclined to check in drying; color light brown, the thick sap-wood nearly white; sometimes used for levers, handles of tools, etc.

294. *Betula alba*, var. *populifolia*, Spach. White Birch.

Distribution: New Brunswick to Delaware; very common in Essex County on lands recently burnt over. A small short-lived tree of rapid growth. Wood light, soft, not strong, close-grained, liable to check in drying, not durable; color light brown, the sap-wood nearly white; largely used in the manufacture of spools, shoe-pegs, wood pulp, etc., for hoop-poles and fuel. The bark and leaves, as well as those of *B. papyrifera* and *B. lenta*, are popularly esteemed as a remedy for various chronic diseases of the skin, bladder, etc., and for rheumatism and gouty complaints; the bark occasionally used domestically in the manufacture of ink.

295. *Betula papyrifera*, Marshall. Canoe Birch. Paper Birch.

Distribution: northern Newfoundland and Labrador to Pennsylvania in the Pacific region south to the Black hills of Dakota, Montana, Washington territory and British Columbia; Salem, Wenham and in other parts of Essex County. Wood light, strong, hard, tough, very close grained, compact; color brown tinged with red, the sapwood nearly white; largely used in the manufacture of spools, shoe-lasts and pegs, in turnery, for fuel, wood-pulp, etc. The very tough, durable bark easily separated into thin layers, impervious to water, is largely used in the manufacture of canoes, tents, etc.

297. *Betula lutea*, Michaux f. Yellow Birch.

Distribution: Newfoundland to North Carolina and Tennessee; frequent in Essex County. Wood heavy, very strong and hard, very close-grained, compact, satiny, susceptible of a beautiful polish; color light brown tinged with red, the heavier sap-wood nearly white; largely used for fuel, in the manufacture of furniture, button and tassel molds, pill and match boxes, and for the hubs of wheels.

298. *Betula nigra*, Linnæus. Red Birch. River Birch.

Distribution: banks of the Merrimac and Spiket rivers, Middlesex and Essex Counties, Massachusetts, to Florida and Texas; along the rivers and near ponds in Lawrence, N. Andover and Georgetown. Wood light, rather hard, strong, close-grained, compact; color brown, the sap-wood much lighter; used in the manufacture of furniture, wooden ware, wooden shoes, ox yokes, etc.

299. *Betula lenta*, Linnæus. Black Birch. Sweet Birch.

Distribution: Newfoundland to Florida and Tennessee; frequent in Essex County. Wood heavy, very strong and hard, close-grained, compact, satiny, susceptible of a beautiful polish; color dark brown tinged with red, the sap-wood light brown or yellow; now largely used in the manufacture of furniture and for fuel, in Nova Scotia and New Brunswick largely in ship-building. "Birch Beer" is obtained by fermenting the saccharine sap of this and perhaps some other species of the genus.

304. *Alnus serrulata*, Willdenow. Smooth Alder.

Distribution: Essex County, Massachusetts to Florida and Texas; a common shrub in Essex County. Wood light, soft, close-grained, compact; color light brown, the sap-wood lighter. A decoction of the bark and leaves, as well as those of *A. incana*, is a popular remedy against impurity of the blood and in the treatment of diarrhœa, etc.

305. *Alnus incana*, Willdenow. Speckled Alder.

Distribution: Newfoundland to base of the Rocky

mountains, south to New England and Nebraska; common in Essex County. Wood light, soft, close-grained, checking in drying; color, light brown, the sap-wood nearly white; preferred and largely used in northern New England in the final baking of bricks, and occasionally, as well as that of *A. serrulata*, in the manufacture of gunpowder.

306. *Salix nigra*, Marshall. Black Willow.

Distribution: southern New Brunswick to Florida and Texas; Pacific region, California and Arizona; frequent near streams and ponds in Essex County. Varying greatly in the size and shape of the leaves, length and habit of the aments, etc. Wood light, soft, weak, close-grained, checking badly in drying; color, brown, the sap-wood nearly white; the tonic and astringent bark use domestically as a popular febrifuge, and containing, in common with that of all the species of the genus, salicylic acid, a powerful anti-pyritic, now successfully used in the treatment of acute cases of gout, rheumatism, typhoid fever, etc.

312. *Salix discolor*, Muhlenberg. Glaucous Willow.

Distribution: Labrador to Delaware and Missouri; common as a large shrub in Essex County. Wood light, soft, close-grained, compact; color, brown streaked with orange, the sap-wood light brown.

318. *Populus tremuloides*, Michaux. Aspen.

Distribution: northern Newfoundland to Alaska; south in the Atlantic region to Pennsylvania and Kentucky; in the Pacific region south to California, Arizona and central Nevada; common in Essex County; the most widely distributed North American tree. Wood light, soft, not strong, close-grained, compact, not durable; color, light brown, the thick sap-wood nearly white; largely manufactured into wood pulp, a substitute for rags in the manufacture of paper; in the Pacific region sometimes used for fuel, flooring, in turnery, etc. A bitter principle of the bark causes its occasional use as a tonic in the treatment of intermittent fever, etc.

319. *Populus grandidentata*, Michaux. Poplar.

Distribution: Nova Scotia to North Carolina and Tennessee; common in Essex County. Wood light, soft, not strong, close-grained, compact; color, light brown, the sap-wood nearly white; largely manufactured into wood-pulp and occasionally used in turnery, for wooden ware, etc.

321. *Populus balsamifera*, Linnæus, var. *candicans*, Gray. Balm of Gilead.

A variety of the common northern tree, rare or unknown in the wild state; much cultivated in Essex County. Wood very light, soft, not strong, close-grained, compact; color, brown, the thick sap-wood nearly white; the buds, as well as those of several other species, covered with a resinous exudation, and occasionally used medicinally as a substitute for turpentine and other balms. The wood is heavier than that of the type (*P. balsamifera*).

329. *Chamæcyparis sphæroidea*, Spach. White Cedar.

Distribution: southern Maine to Florida, and Mississippi; swamps in Essex County, frequent. Wood very light and soft, close-grained, compact, easily worked, very durable in contact with the soil; color, light brown tinged with red, growing darker with exposure, the sap-wood lighter; largely used in boat-building, for wooden ware, cooperage, shingles, interior finish, telegraph and fence posts, railway ties, etc. Along the Atlantic coast from New Jersey southward, lumber is manufactured from buried trunks of this species dug from peat swamps.

339. *Juniperus Virginiana*, Linnæus. Red Cedar.
Distribution : New Brunswick to Minnesota, south to
Florida and Texas ; in the Pacific region, Colorado to
British Columbia ; in Utah, Nevada and Arizona, rare and
local ; common on sterile hills in Essex County ; the most
widely distributed tree among the North American Coniferæ. Wood light, soft, not strong, brittle, very close
and straight-grained, compact, easily worked, very durable
in contact with the soil ; odorous : color, dull red, the sap-
wood nearly white ; largely used for posts, sills, railway
ties, interior finish, cabinet making, and almost exclusively
for lead pencils. A decoction of the leaves is occasionally
used as a substitute for *savine cerete*, and an infusion of
the berries as a diuretic.

347. *Pinus Strobus*, Linnæus. White Pine.
Distribution : Newfoundland, the valley of the Winnipeg river, south to Pennsylvania, and along the Alleghany mountains to northern Georgia ; abundant in Essex
County. Wood light, soft, not strong, very close,
straight-grained, compact, easily worked, susceptible of
a beautiful polish ; color, light brown, often slightly
tinged with red, the sap-wood nearly white ; more largely
manufactured into lumber, shingles, laths, etc., than that
of any other North American tree ; the common and
most valuable building material of the northern states ; .
largely used in cabinet-making, for interior finish, and in
the manufacture of matches, wooden ware, and for many
domestic purposes. Coniferin, a glucoside principle, has
been discovered in the cambium layer of this and several
other species of Coniferæ.

358. *Pinus resinosa*, Aiton. Red Pine. Norway Pine.
Distribution : Newfoundland to the valley of the Winnipeg river, south to Massachusetts, northern Pennsylvania, Michigan, and central Minnesota ; one grove in

Boxford and scattered trees in adjoining towns in Essex County. Wood light, not strong, hard, rather coarse-grained, compact; color, light red, the sap-wood yellow or often almost white; largely manufactured into lumber and used for all purposes of construction, flooring, piles, etc.

371. *Pinus rigida*, Miller. Pitch Pine.

Distribution: New Brunswick to Lake Ontario, south to Georgia and Kentucky; common in Essex County. Wood, light, soft, not strong, brittle, coarse-grained. compact; color, light brown or red, the thick sap-wood yellow or often nearly white; largely used for fuel, charcoal, and occasionally manufactured into coarse lumber.

382. *Picea nigra*, Link. Black Spruce.

Distribution: Newfoundland to Hudson Bay, south to Pennsylvania, Wisconsin and Minnesota, and to the high peaks of North Carolina; occasional in Essex County. Wood light, soft, not strong, close, straight-grained, compact, satiny; color, light red or often nearly white, the sap-wood lighter; largely manufactured into lumber, used in construction, for ship-building, piles, posts, railway ties, etc. Essence of spruce, prepared by boiling the young branches of this species, is used in the manufacture of spruce beer, a popular beverage.

387. *Tsuga Canadensis*, Carriere. Hemlock.

Distribution: Nova Scotia to Lake Temiscaming, and southwest to Wisconsin; south to Delaware and Alabama; abundant in Essex County. Wood light, soft, not strong, brittle, coarse, crooked-grained, difficult to work, liable to wind-shake and splinter, not durable; color, light brown tinged with red or often nearly white, the sap-wood somewhat darker; largely manufactured into coarse lumber and used in construction in outside finish, railway ties, etc.; two varieties, red and white, produced apparently under precisely similar conditions of growth, are recognized by lumbermen. The bark, rich in tannin, is the principal material used in the northern states in tanning leather, and yields a fluid extract sometimes used medicinally as a powerful astringent. Canada or hemlock pitch, prepared from the resinous secretions of this species, is used in the preparation of stimulating plasters, etc.

401. *Larix Americana*, Michaux. Larch.

Distribution: northern Newfoundland and northwest to the valley of the Mackenzie river within the Arctic circle; south to northern Pennsylvania and Minnesota; occasional in swamps in Essex County. Wood heavy, hard, very strong, rather coarse-grained, compact, durable in contact with the soil; color, light brown, the sap-wood nearly white; preferred and largely used for the upper knees of vessels, for ship timbers, fence posts, telegraph poles, railway ties, etc. The inner bark of the closely allied European larch is recommended in the treatment of chronic catarrhal affections of the pulmonary and urinary passages; probably that of the American species would be equally efficaceous.

LIST OF CERTAIN NORTH AMERICAN TREES POSSESSING COMMERCIAL VALUE WHICH MAY BE CULTIVATED SUCCESSFULLY IN ESSEX COUNTY.

Fraxinus quadrangulata (Ash), from Michigan, etc.

Catalpa speciosa (Western Catalpa), valley of the Mississippi river.

Ulmus racemosa (Rock Elm), western Atlantic states.

Juglans nigra (Black Walnut), western Atlantic states.

Carya sulcata (Western Shagbark Hickory), western Atlantic states.

Quercus imbricaria (Shingle Oak), western Atlantic states.

Quercus macrocarpa (Overcup Oak), western and northern Atlantic states.

Picea alba (White Spruce), northern America.

Pseudotsuga Douglasii (Douglas Fir), Rocky mountains.

EXPLANATIONS OF THE TABLES.

TABLE A. The first and second columns give the relative fuel value of the wood of such species of the native trees of Essex County as have been actually tested, considered first by volume and second by the weight of the wood. The figures here given show the relative standing of these species considered in connection with all the woods tested for this purpose, of which there were seventy specimens of sixty-four different species of trees. The standing of any one tree as compared with other Essex County trees may of course be seen by taking the numbers as given in a rising scale and making no account of omissions. The five columns of figures which follow show the relative standing of Essex County trees when considered in connection with all species of trees tested, about three hundred in number, as regards their weight, approximate fuel value, elasticity, transverse strength and resistance to longitudinal pressure. The relative standing of Essex County trees compared with each other will be seen in the same manner as given above.

TABLE B. The figures here given are derived from the actual tests of specimens furnished by the Academy from Essex County. The blocks used for specific gravity determinations "were made one hundred millimeters long, about thirty-five millimeters square and were dried at one hundred degrees centigrade until they ceased to lose weight." The unit in these determinations is an equal volume of water. The ash determinations were made by "burning small dried blocks in a muffle furnace at a low temperature." The figures indicate the percentage of ash by weight in the specimens tested.

The specimens used in testing for transverse strength "were made four centimeters square and placed on bearings exactly one meter apart." The specimens were placed upright and "pressure was applied by means of an iron rod twelve millimeters in radius acting midway between supports." The figures give the pressure in kilograms required to break the specimen. The tests for longitudinal compression were made upon blocks "four centimeters square and thirty-two centimeters (eight diameters) long. They were placed between the platforms of the machine and pressure was gradually applied until they failed." As before the figures given are in kilograms.

TABLE C. In this table will be found the figures for the tests of such species which, although becoming trees in certain regions of their distribution, are only shrubs in Essex County, and a few others which are large shrubs throughout their entire distribution. Some of these last, at first included in the census list of trees, were finally thrown out. The figures for these tests are taken from a paper entitled "The specific gravity, ash, etc., of certain shrubs and exotic trees found growing in the United States," by S. P. Sharples, read before the Boston Society of Natural History, May 16, 1883, and printed in the society's Proceedings. The explanations given above for Table B apply also to Table C.

TABLE A. RELATIVE FUEL VALUE, STRENGTH, ETC., OF THE WOODS OF THE NATIVE TREES OF ESSEX COUNTY, MASS.

	Relative actual fuel value among 70 spm. of 64 important woods.		Rel. weight among all species tested.	Relative position among 300 species tested.			
	By vol.	By wg't.		Approximate fuel value.	Elasticity.	Ultimate transverse strength.	Ultimate resistance to longitudinal pressure.
Tilia Americana, *Bass Wood or Linden*....			364	246	161	241	240
†Acer saccharinum, *Sugar or Rock Maple.*	23	19	178	117	9	18	30
Acer dasycarpum, *White or Silver Maple.*			301	192	59	53	113
Acer rubrum, *Red or Swamp Maple*......			240	154	117	121	133
Rhus typhina, *Staghorn Sumach*..........			377				
Robinia Pseudacacia, *Locust*..............	29	58	138	87	19	3	12
Robinia viscosa, *Clammy Locust*..........			83				
Prunus serotina, *Wild black Cherry*.....			260	164	153	115	61
Amelanchier Canadensis. *June Berry*.....			97	57	34	24	19
Hamamelis Virginica, *Witch Hazel*........			185				
Nyssa sylvatica, *Tupelo*..................			227	141	178	112	125
Fraxinus Americana, *White Ash*...........	36	24	206	130	91	106	121
Fraxinus pubescens, *Red Ash*........			237	151	182	101	162
Fraxinus sambucifolia, *Black Ash*........			232	149	142	125	175
Sassafras officinale, *Sassafras*..........			314	202	273	235	221
Ulmus fulva, *Slippery Elm*................			170	111	110	101	66
Ulmus Americana, *Elm*..........	16	26	212	136	205	110	146
Celtis occidentalis, *Nettle Tree*...........			144	94	229	135	178
Platanus occidentalis, *Button Wood*......	42	40	271	173	146	222	144
Juglans cinerea, *Butter Nut*...........			397	270	181	238	205
Carya alba, *Shagbark Hickory*.............	*10	*48	64	36	12	11	27
Carya pocina, *Pig Nut*...................	10	53	76	42	92	31	43
Carya amara, *Bitter Nut*...................	27	56	114	71	86	30	78
Quercus alba, *White Oak*.............	17	28	124	76	104	85	82
Quercus bicolor, *Swamp White Oak*......			107	60	131	81	102
Quercus rubra, *Red Oak*.........	24	37	207	129	48	63	83
Quercus tinctoria, *Black Oak*...........	37	64	167	106	81	44	92
Quercus coccinea, *Scarlet Oak*............			136	84	65	38	87
Castanea vulgaris, var. Americana, *Chestnut*........................	56	43	365	247	152	184	222
Fagus ferruginea, *Beech*....	31	57	184	120	32	18	120
Ostrya Virginica, *Hop Hornbeam*........			73	40	15	23	64
Carpinus Caroliniana, *Iron Wood*........			145	92	43	18	96
Betula alba, var. populifolia, *White or Gray Birch*................	40	39	267	168	214	140	254
Betula papyrifera, *Paper or Canoe Birch.*	39	34	251	159	18	37	109
Betula lutea, *Yellow Birch*.............			204	127	3	5	29
Betula nigra, *Red or River Birch*........			266	170	58	66	157
Betula lenta, *Black Birch.*			111	64	10	9	31
Alnus incana, *Speckled Alder*.............			355				
Salix nigra, *Black Willow*.			371				
Populus tremuloides, *Aspen*..............	63	20	400	275	180	198	266
Populus grandidentata, *Large toothed Aspen*......			350	234	108	169	243
Populus Balsamifera, var. candicans, *Balm of Gilead*..			390	264	215	232	286
Chamæcyparis sphæroidea, *White Cedar*..			423	296	294	281	294
Juniperus Virginiana, *Red Cedar*........			325	212	238	158	177
Pinus Strobus, *White Pine*................	66	21	408	282	154	225	212
Pinus resinosa, *Red Pine*................	49	23	332	217	51	131	140
Pinus rigida, *Pitch Pine*........	9	1	308	197	261	158	245
Picea nigra, *Black Spruce*................	64	51	357	237	60	156	193
Tsuga Canadensis, *Hemlock*........	61	25	384	258	135	171	219
Larix Americana, *Larch*.................	26	29	239	153	23	90	58

† Only var. nigrum tested.   * Average of two specimens tested.

**III OF REPO
STS.**

RKS.

:plitting at er

. . . .

. . . .

. . . .

. . . .

. . . .

. . . .

. . . .

. . . .

. . . .

. . . .

. . . .

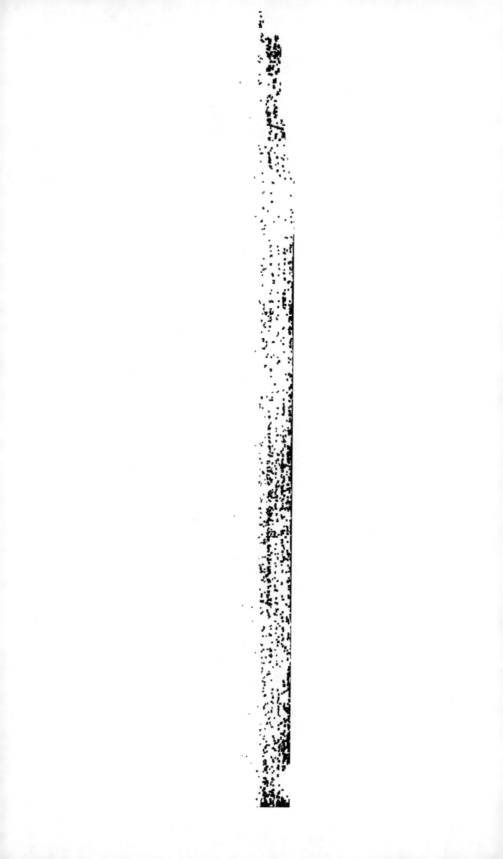

(3)

PROCEEDINGS OF THE TRUSTEES.

July 6, 1885.   The day appointed for the semi-annual meeting of the Trustees occurring on the Fourth of July, a legal holiday, the meeting was duly called to be held this day at nine o'clock A. M.   The following members of the Board were present, namely, the Vice President, the Secretary, the Treasurer and Mr. Peabody.

The meeting was called to order by the Vice President, Dr. Henry Wheatland and, by vote, the reading of the records of the previous meeting was dispensed with.   It was also voted that the Director be requested to attend this meeting.

The Treasurer in behalf of the building committee read a report of work done to date, whereupon it was voted: that the action of the Treasurer, as herein set forth, be approved and the report placed on file.

Voted: that the agreement between the Trustees of the Academy and the Trustees of the estate of the late Francis Peabody be approved and that the Treasurer be authorized to sign it for the Board.

Voted: that the flat roof and truss, as shown on the first plan for the addition to East India Marine Hall, submitted by the architect, Mr. Stone, be adopted.

Voted: that the building committee be empowered to act, and that the finance committee be empowered to meet the required payments in such a manner as they may deem most advisable.

Voted: that the Treasurer be authorized to lay a new floor in the exhibition hall of the Museum.

After some discussion relative to the addition to the building, the Board adjourned *sine die*.

Attest,
ABNER C. GOODELL, JR., *Secretary.*

April 21, 1886. The annual meeting of the Trustees, adjourned to the call of the President from January 2, at which date no quorum was present, was held this day at 10 o'clock A. M., at the rooms of the Academy.

Present, Messrs. Endicott, Nichols, Cogswell, Robinson and Wheatland. The President in the chair. In the absence of the Secretary, Dr. Wheatland was chosen Secretary *pro tem.*

The records of the previous meeting were read and accepted.

The Treasurer's report was read and accepted.

The Director's report was read and accepted.

Mr. Robinson read his report on the work of the Academy, condition of the Museum, list of accessions, number of visitors, etc. The report was accepted.

Voted : that the appropriations for the year be the same as for the previous year.

The following officers were chosen for the year and until others be elected in their place :

WILLIAM C. ENDICOTT, *President.*
HENRY WHEATLAND, *Vice President.*
JOHN ROBINSON, *Treasurer.*
ABNER C. GOODELL, JR., *Secretary.*

Finance Committee, the President, Treasurer and Dr. Cogswell.

Executive Committee, the President, Vice President, Treasurer, Secretary and Dr. Nichols.

Voted : that all matters in relation to the shares of the Salem Athenæum held by the Academy be referred to a committee consisting of the President, Vice President and Treasurer, with full powers.

The Board then adjourned *sine die.*

Attest,
HENRY WHEATLAND, *Secretary pro tem.*

Report of the Treasurer of the Peabody Academy

Dr.   CASH.

1885.

Jan. 31.   To Balance of account this date   -   .   .   . $ 1,881 24
      " Rec'd for F. W. Putnam's note,   .   .   .   4,250 00
      "   " Loan Salem National Bank,   .   .   .   10,000 00 $16,131 24

Receipts for the year ending January 31, 1886.

Rents Museum Building	. . . . . .		825 00
" King	do	. . . .	2,485 27
" Hubon	do	. . . .	330 00
" Cook	do	. . . .	264 00

Receipts for Coupons	Indianapolis & Vincennes R. R.			700 00
"	"	"	Del. & Hudson Canal Co.	280 00
"	"	"	Mobile & Ohio R. R. . .	300 00
"	"	"	Chicago City . . .	700 00
"	"	"	Michigan Central R. R. .	400 00
"	"	"	Kansas City, St. Jo. & C. Bluffs R. R.	850 00
"	"	"	Chicago & E. Illinois R. R.	180 00
"	"	"	Cincinnati, Sandusky and Cleveland R. R. . . .	540 00
"	"	"	Burlington, Cedar Rapids & Northern R. R. . . .	250 00
"	"	Dividends Salem Nat'l. Bank . .		350 00
"	"	"	Fort Wayne & Jackson R. R.	363 00
"	"	"	Chicago, Burlington & Quincy R. R.	406 25
"	"	Tax returned on Bank stock . .		94 74
Receipts at Museum,	. . . . . .			57 96 $8,376 22

                                                         24,507 46

To Balance brought forward 548 27

                                     JOHN ROBINSON,

SALEM, JANUARY 31, 1886.   *Treasurer.*

of Science of Salem for the year ending January 31, 1886.

CASH.   Cr.

Investments for the year ending January 31, 1886.

By paid King Building Improvement   .   . $2,950 63
"   "   on account of Academy Hall   .   .   13,822 18 $16,272 81

Expenditures for the year ending January 31, 1886.

By paid Salaries at the Museum $3,900 00
"   "   Permanent additions to specimens in the
      Museum   .   .   .   330 00
"   "   Other Museum expenses   .   .   .   621 90 $4,851 90

"   "   State, County and City tax   .   .   . $498 30
"   "   Book-keeper and care of real estate   .   300 00
"   "   City of Salem water tax   .   .   .   44 10
"   "   King Building repairs, Janitor and fuel   396 06
"   "   Cook House repairs 25 56
"   "   Hard wood floor in Museum   .   .   300 00
"   "   Museum repairs and Insurance   .   .   367 62
"   "   Alterations in E. I. M. Hall   .   .   408 64
"   "   Permanent additions to furniture and
      cases in Museum 90 00
"   "   Publication account 349 30
"   "   Sundries, Express, Box rent, etc.   .   54 90 $2,834 48

"   Balance to new account   .   .   .   548 27

                                      $24,507 46

Property Statement.*

Permanent Fund, January 31, 1886,		$100,000.00
Reserve Fund, January 31, 1886,		11,424.36
		$111,424.36

Invested as follows:

10,000	City of Chicago Water Loan Bonds 7 per cent, due 1894,	$9,547 22
10,000	Indianapolis & Vincennes R. R. Bonds 7 per cent, due 1908,	8,500 00
9,000	Cincinnati, Sandusky & Cleveland R. R. Bonds 6 per cent, due 1900,	9,348 84
5,000	Michigan Central R. R. Bonds 8 per cent, due 1890,	5,410 00
5,000	Scioto Valley Railroad Bonds 7 per cent, due 1896,	5,164 30
5,000	Kansas City, St. Jo. & C. Bluffs R. R. Bonds 7 per cent, due 1907,	5,490 31
5,000	Burlington, Cedar Rapids & No. R. R. Bonds 5 per cent, due 1934,	4,595 83
5,000	Mobile & Ohio Railroad Bonds 6 per cent, due 1891,	5,139 08
4,000	Delaware & Hudson Canal Co. Bonds 7 per cent. due 1917,	4,040 88
3,000	Chicago & Eastern Illinois R. R. Bonds 6 per cent, due 1907,	3,007 33
50 shares Salem National Bank of Salem,		5,944 86
50 "	Chicago, Burlington & Quincy R. R.	6,131 25
66 "	Fort Wayne & Jackson R. R.	4,605 56
	King Building, Essex St., Salem,	28,750 63
	Hubon House, Charter St., "	3,000 00
	Cook House " " "	2,200 00
	Deposit Salem National Bank,	548 27
		$111,424 36

*Not including the East India Marine Hall property, museum fittings, furniture, library nor collections, which, exclusive of the collections received as permanent deposits from the East India Marine Society and Essex Institute may be roughly estimated at upwards of $60,000.

MUSEUM REPORTS.

I.

REPORT OF EDWARD S. MORSE, DIRECTOR.

THE Director would respectfully submit his report for the year 1885 to the Trustees of the Peabody Academy of Science.

During the past year the time of the Director has been mainly occupied in the preparation and completion of his work on "Japanese Homes and their Surroundings." The manuscript went to the printers in August, and the book was issued December 15. Through the kindness of Messrs. Ticknor and Co., the Academy has been enabled to issue this work as the second volume of its memoirs and copies are to be distributed to all its foreign correspondents.

For a number of years the Academy has been in receipt of exchanges from home and foreign Societies, many of them being publications of great value for which no adequate return has been made. The judicious arrangement whereby Dr. Abbott's work on "Primitive Industry" was secured as an issue of the Academy, which partly made up the indebtedness to these societies that have so long and so faithfully continued their contributions, also had the effect to increase the influx of exchanges from abroad. It is believed that the present memoir will still further reduce our indebtedness. As to the appropriateness of this work as a publication of the Academy the director for obvious reasons cannot speak. He may be permitted to say, however, that the publishers have received letters from M. Burty, the eminent French oriental scholar and from other eminent authorities requesting copies of the work for review in ethnological journals.   While it is true that the work could not have appeared so promptly had not the Trustees taken the liberal view that the preparation of such a volume was a proper and legitimate work of the institution, the Academy is indebted to the publishers for their interest and assistance and to the University Press for the perfect way in which the mechanical work has been done.

For a number of years the want of an assistant to specially care for the exchanges, properly enter them, as well as to record all accessions to the Museum, and the miscellaneous clerical work required has been keenly felt. By the appointment of Mr. Arthur R. Stone as Librarian this work and much other work which had before been divided, have been brought under one head. Mr. Stone on assuming his special duties, as Librarian, visited the principal libraries of Boston and Cambridge and familiarized himself with the best methods of recording and arranging the books and exchanges, and the work accomplished in this department is shown in his Report of the year which is herewith submitted.

The plans for the new building, which were presented to the Trustees in the spring and approved by them, were placed in the hands of Messrs. Stone, Carpenter and Willson, architects, and the details of finish and decoration were perfected by them.

To Prof. Geo. L. Vose, of the Institute of Technology, the Academy is indebted for advice and assistance in connection with the plans for the roof trusses and girders.

Only words of praise can be given to the masons, Messrs. Mack and to the carpenters, Messrs. Hamilton and Balcomb, for the honest and faithful performance of their respective contracts. The work has been under the daily supervision of Mr. Robinson, and many improvements have been suggested by him as the work progressed. The alterations and changes which have been made in the main building have also been under his direction. To-day the Academy finds itself in possession of two large and spacious exhibition halls, the new one as nearly fire-proof within and without as it was possible to make it; a beautiful and convenient lecture hall; ample and commodious rooms for offices, class and museum work. When the new exhibition hall is completed no further expense will be required in this direction for years to come.

The Director would specially urge, however, that some method of steam heating be introduced at the earliest possible moment. As a matter of safety, the source of heat should originate from a single fire. It is an urgent necessity that the arctic temperature of the present exhibition hall may be tempered in some degree, as it is not only uncomfortable but perilous to remain there long during the months of winter, and practically useless to attempt work on the case arrangement of specimens. Then too, with the recurrence of warm days after cold spells, the condensation of moisture on the cases causes much trouble.

Owing to the confusion and dirt incident to the constructions and changes, special work on the collections has been greatly interfered with; nevertheless a good deal has been accomplished in this direction, as will be seen by Mr. Robinson's report.

It is hoped and believed that the income from the lecture hall will pay the interest on the cost of its construction and perhaps be a source of some additional revenue.

The last annual Report which was issued early in the year contained a report compiled by Mr. Robinson from the 10th U. S. Census giving the tests of those woods found in Essex County, the examples of which were furnished by the Academy and a duplicate set of these specimens illustrating the experiments are now in the collections. This report was sent to all our correspondents and the result has been to nearly double our accessions to the library.

The Academy has to deplore the loss of William Dolan, Esq., of Hong Kong. Mr. Dolan has been a good friend to the Academy and has made valuable contributions to its cabinets, and at the time of his death had been making collections to fill certain desiderata in the Chinese Department.

EDWARD S. MORSE, Director.

East India Marine Hall,
Feb. 1, 1886.

II.

REPORT OF THE WORK OF THE ACADEMY AND THE CONDITION OF THE MUSEUM WITH A LIST OF ACCESSIONS, FOR THE YEAR 1885.

BY JOHN ROBINSON, TREASURER, IN CHARGE OF THE MUSEUM.

WORK ON MUSEUM.

THE re-arrangement of the zoological collections which has been in progress for some time was continued during the spring and summer months, type collections, illustrating the families of mollusks and insects being placed in the central floor case on the western side of the hall. The work on these collections, owing to the care required for the selection of specimens, occupied all the time of the assistants during the early portion of the year.

The minerals and fossils, packed in boxes since 1867, have been assorted into the cases recently prepared for them. This has been done by Mr. Sears, with the assistance of Rev. B. F. McDaniel, who gratuitously devoted a considerable time to the work.

Beginning in April and continuing through the season, Mr. Sears made systematic collections of Essex County plants, adding important desiderata to the herbarium which, as heretofore, has been continually used for class work by the Botanical Section and frequently consulted by others. Some work has been done upon the collections of Essex County birds and mammals and also upon various portions of the ethnological collections.

The alcoholic specimens stored in the basement have been thoroughly examined and assorted with the assistance of several specialists connected with the Museum of Comparative Zoology at Cambridge. Such as were considered of special importance to the Academy have been placed in fresh alcohol, while others have been transferred to Cambridge and a large number of duplicates have been disposed of for study at Wellesley College and otherwise distributed.

LECTURES AND CLASS WORK.

The lectures on Mineralogy by Rev. Benj. F. McDaniel, begun in December, 1884, were continued through the winter, supplemented by a series of excursions conducted during the summer months, the parties visiting Marblehead and other points of interest to students of mineralogy. The lectures were attended by a class of twenty-six and the excursions by a class of twelve persons.

The Botanical Section continued its meetings with twenty-one regular attendants. The principal families of native plants were studied, different members taking charge of the meetings.

Mr. Morse has addressed several meetings at the Essex Institute and the Marblehead Farmers' Club, outside his regular work, and Mr. Sears has spoken before the Danvers, Marblehead and other local organizations on botanical subjects. The Treasurer has also read papers and spoken on several occasions in the county during the year.

PUBLICATIONS.

The volume, including the annual report for 1884 and the report on the results of the tests made upon the collection of Essex County Woods, was forwarded to all the Academy's correspondents about the first of May. The second volume of the Academy's memoirs, being the work on "Japanese Homes and their Surroundings," by the Director, has recently been received from the printer, and will be distributed at once to all foreign correspondents of the Academy.

IMPROVEMENTS IN THE BUILDING.

The building of the addition to East India Marine Hall has necessitated several alterations in the old lecture room. One chimney has been removed and the partition between this and the dark store room has been taken away, thus throwing what was originally three rooms into one large one. This change increases the room for the herbarium and collections of shells and gives much better accommodation for the meetings of the East India Marine Society for which the Academy, by its agreement with that society, has to provide, and in addition the rear hallway and office have been painted and papered. In the museum a new, hard pine floor has been laid, an improvement much needed, as the dust from the old and badly worn soft pine floor occasioned much trouble.

ACCESSIONS.

The museum accessions for the year number one hundred and seventy-five separate entries from one hundred and twenty-seven institutions and individuals, and aggregate about twenty-five hundred specimens distributed as follows :

Botanical specimens, Essex Co., .	150
Pre-historic relics, Essex Co., . .	1,200
Ethnological specimens, . . .	300
Minerals, ...	250
Insects, ...	200
Miscellaneous, ...	400
	2,500

The Academy has been fortunate in securing a fine specimen of *Dermatochelys coriacea*, or leather backed turtle, from the waters of the county and also a very large specimen of the common pond turtle during the year. Among the ethnological specimens received, the objects from Japan and China from Mrs. Chas. Parker, collected by Alfred Greenough, the Chinese dentist's apparatus and casts of compressed Chinese feet from Dr. G. O. Rogers, the hammock and dress from B. S. Conrad of Demerara, the objects from Africa from Edward Ropes, Jr., and the model of a Manila boat from Capt. J. Warren Luscomb are deserving of special notice.

PORTRAITS.

Several oil portraits of interest connected with the early commercial history of Salem and members of the East India Marine Society have been received during the year including those of William Story, William Brown, William Fettyplace and Joseph Pratt and, in addition, a lithographic portrait of Lt. Jesse Smith and photographs of other members of the Society.

VISITORS.

The number of visitors to the museum for the year was 42,579 being an increase of 4,328 over the number in

1884 and 6,000 over the average for fifteen years. This increase is undoubtedly due to the improved horse railroad facilities which have recently been developed in the vicinity of Salem.

Arranged by quarters the visitors for the past two years are as follows :—

	1884	1885
Jan. 1 to March 31,	7,822	6,517
April 1 to June 30,	8,129	9,205
July 1 to Sept. 30,	13,796	16,559
Oct. 1 to Dec. 31,	8,504	10,298
	38,251	42,579

The largest number on single days were :—

Feb. 23, Celebration of Washington's birthday	272
April 2, Fast day	544
June 20, Party from Newton	413
June 23, Barnum's circus in Salem	408
July 4	834
July 15, Party from Dover, N. H.	970
Oct. 8, Centennial anniversary of Salem Cadets	725

Owing to the confusion arising from the building operations during the year and the continual interruptions occasioned by the presence of workmen about the building, the results of the year's work have been materially interfered with, yet considerable has been accomplished and, at least, the condition of the building and collections has been much improved.

Respectfully submitted,

JOHN ROBINSON, *Treas.*,

in charge of the Museum.

East India Marine Hall,
February 1, 1886.

ACCESSIONS TO THE MUSEUM

Almy, Jas. F.   Straw carpet loom, bundles of straw, shop sign, photographs, etc., from China.

Arrington, Stephen W.   Water scorpion.

Barker, Wm. G.   Cocoon of Attacus cecropia.

Bartlett, John W.   Globular basalt, Indian implements.

Bell, John H.   Stone resembling a shell from Nahant.

Bolles, Rev. E. C.   Pumice from Kracatoa eruption, marl, wood paper.

Brigham, A. P.   Sand from Mt. Desert.

Brigham, Mrs. L. F.   Photograph of Aug. Perry, member E. I. M. Soc.

Brooks, H. M.   Large jar, China ; notices of East India Marine Soc.

Brooks, Miss Margarette W.   Paper fish Japan, poisoned arrow.

Cabot, Geo. D., Lawrence.   Section pillar from the ruins of the Pemberton Mills.

Call, Wm. H.   Shot found in the old Phillips school house.

Conckling, H. A., Hamilton.   Large spider.

Conrad, B. S., Georgetown, Demerara.   "Que yu" woman's dress, Carib hammock, snake nuts.

Conway, Wm. H.   Abnormal potato.

Couper, W. Audley, Marietta, Ga.   Opossum with young in pouch.

Curtis, Chas., Boxford.   Young turtle.

Curtis, Francis, Topsfield.   Large hornet's nest.

Curwen, Jas. B.   Mineral.

Dennis, Edith L.   Collection of butterflies.

Derby, Miss Mary.   Old paper and original engraving by Hogarth.

Dodge, Clarence P. Red bat and young.

Dodge, Isaiah H., No. Beverly. California cucumber, yellow corn, etc.

Essex Institute. Collection of Indian relics.

Farrell, H. F. E. Juglans nigra from Salem.

Fisk, Mrs. J. B. Ancient clog from Londonderry about 1776.

Fitzgerald, Richard. Specimens of pumice and soap stone.

Fitzpatrick, Maggie N. Collection of butterflies.

Follansbee, P. B., Andover. Stones from glacial drift.

Fowler, S. P., Danvers. Tree toad.

French, Arthur B., Boston. Six Japanese photographs.

Friend, Chas. Abnormal lobster claws.

Gardner, Arthur W. Capricorn beetle.

Gardner, Mrs. Henry. Specimens of bamboo.

Gardner, Wm. D. Portion of nest of white ant from house in Salem.

Goldthwait, J. W. Web-fringed gunnard, insects, etc.

Gould, Walter, Ipswich. Bufo Americana.

Grover, Mrs. Chas., Gloucester Essex County plants.

Haddock, Dr. Chas., Beverly. Young night heron.

Harley, Claude B. "Hop Toy," opium box, China.

Harriman, H. N., Georgetown. Water scorpion.

Honeycomb, Mrs. Military hat, plume, etc.

Horner, Mrs. C. N. S., Georgetown. Dried plants.

Humphrey, Edwin. White wax from Sze-chuen province, China.

Hunt, T. F. Umbrella, box and cloth from India.

Huntington, A. L. Copper from old mine Lake Superior.

Johnson, Abbott, Wenham. Pond turtle weighing 50 lbs., collected by Mr. Wesell.

Jewett, Thos. E. Thyreus Abbotti.

Kimball, Joel, Beverly. Section of Sumach tree.

Kimball, Mrs. M. W., Wenham. Variegated trifolium.

King, H. F. Fungus from an old elm tree.

Kirk, James. Brown bat.

Kyes, Miss, Worcester. Insects.

Lake, David, Peabody. Eggs of "Aphis lion. "

Langford, John, Gloucester.   Indian sinker.

Larrabee, E. C.   Abnormal hen's eggs.

Lee, F. H.   Stem of Aristolochia sipho.

Loring, Miss Ruth, Boston.   Doll from China.

Lowell, Percival, Boston.   Thief's lantern, set of dominoes and photographs from Korea.

Luscomb, J. Warren.   Model of sailing canoe from Philippine Isl. and centipede.

Mack, Dr. Wm.   Fruit of pepper tree from California.

Maloon, Mrs. Lucy M.   Fungus from Ship Rock.

Manning, Henry.   Larva of fly.

McLoud, Mrs. P. E. A.   Minerals from California.

Miller, Louis F.   Shells.

Millett, Nath. H.   Old French print, 1793.

Mooney, Chas.   Red bat.

Murray, Henry.   Larva of large moth.

Newcomb, R. L.   Domestic turkey, Yemshik's pipe from Siberia.

Nichols, Andrew, jr.   Barnacle on rock weed from Beverly.

Nichols, Fred K.   Abnormal flower of Clematis.

Nichols, Thos. B.   Rose water bottle from Persia, and large moth.

O'Brien, Daniel J.   Grant medal.

Paige, Chas. A.   Alligator from Florida.

Paige, I. M.   Butterfly from the Southern States.

Parker, Mr. and Mrs. Chas. H., Boston.   Ethnological objects from Japan and South Sea Islands, from the collection of the late Alfred Greenough.

Patch, Nathan W., Beverly.   Indian pipe and coral from Beverly.

Peabody, J. B., jr., Middleton.   Larva of moth.

Perkins, Chas., Wakefield.   Indian implement.

Perkins, Solon.   Asbestos from Danville, Province Quebec.

Pitts, D. & Co.   Iron pyrites.

Plummer, Miss Mary N.   Plants.

Pratt, John J., Wakefield.   Portrait of Jos. Pratt, captain of Grand Turk.

Reed, Addison. Red bat and young.

Roberts, Mrs. C. C. Spider.

Robinson, Mary and Lucy. Japanese toy bird and Jinrikisha, beetle.

Rogers, Dr. G. O., Boston. Models of tomb, casts of Chinese feet, dentists' outfit from China.

Ropes, Chas. F. Pickerel from Wenham pond.

Ropes, Edward, jr. Somali knife, tobacco pouch and other ethnological objects, from Zanzibar, dried ferns from St. Helena.

Ropes, Willis H. Tree toad.

Russell, Miss Mary C. Northern Phalrope, Cape Cod.

Russell, Peter S. Hornet's nest and spider's nest.

Rugg, Daniel, Ipswich. Indian bead from Ipswich.

Saunders, Miss Mary T. Shells and gorget from South Sea Isl., and autograph letters of botanists.

Sears, John H. Wood frog, Indian implements, Essex Co. plants, animals, etc.

Sears, Robert K., Danvers. Head of razor-billed Auk.

Silsbee, Wm. H. Young skate.

Smith, Ernest. Attacus cecropia.

Smith, Miss F. C. Caddis fly larva from Princeton, Mass.

Smith, Miss Sarah E. Lithographic portrait of Lt. Jesse Smith.

Smith & Parker. Leather backed turtle.

Stickney, J. W. Model of Lafayette Hose carriage.

Stone, Arthur R. Echinoderm from Washington Territory.

Stone, Frank. Ground squirrel from Oakland, Oregon.

Story, Estate of Eliza. Portrait of Capt. William Story.

Sutton, Mrs. William. Indian gouge, Ipswich.

Tagdell, H. Insects.

Temple, Arthur S. Minerals from California.

Thayer, E. S. Insects.

Thayer, Oliver, jr. Ethnological specimens.

Thorner, John C. Abnormal tomato.

True, Eben, Salisbury. Sabbatia stellaris.

Upham, W. P., Peabody. Insect, minerals, salamander, etc.

Verry, Daniel W., Peabody. Mole crickets.

Vickary, N., Lynn. Indian implement, intergrowth in Hornbeam tree, Essex Co. animals, etc.

Ward, Samuel. Slug (Limax).

Ward & Howell, Rochester, N. Y. Ethnological objects.

Welch, Wm. L. Fossil shark's tooth from So. Carolina.

Whipple, Albert. Veronica.

Whipple, C. Prescott. Peg wood from Upper Bartlett, N. H., printed memorial of Com. Lawrence.

Wiggin, Mrs. Andrew J., So. Peabody. Twin apples, etc.

Willcomb, J., jr. Indian implements.

Yu Kil Chun. Korean envelope.

Fujiyama Co. Set of Japanese dolls.

III.

REPORT ON THE LIBRARY; ITS CONDITION AND ACCESSIONS FOR THE YEAR 1885.

BY ARTHUR R. STONE, LIBRARIAN.

On account of the limited size of the library and the fact that the annual accessions are regularly received from comparatively few sources, chiefly exchanges from foreign and American scientific societies, it is thought better, for the present, to adhere to the method of arranging the books by countries and societies rather than by subjects.

During the year a new exchange list has been made up in conformity with the catalogue prepared the previous season, the American and foreign exchanges being kept in separate volumes.

By a change recently made at the Smithsonian Institution, foreign exchange receipts are no longer forwarded, so that all accessions are now acknowledged directly upon their receipt at the Academy. This is done upon postal card blanks and at the close of the year the printed report is forwarded to each contributor.

The accessions for the year have been as follows :—

Bound volumes, . .	38
Part serials, . . .	557
Pamphlets, . . .	88
	683

This does not include numerous catalogues, papers, etc., which do not strictly come within the scope of our library and which, as heretofore, have been deposited with the Essex Institute.

It will be seen that the accessions for the year were nearly double the number (384) received in 1884, a result doubtless of the resumption of its publications on the part of the Academy.

By a rearrangement of the cases and the addition of some new ones, the books have all been reclassified and more conveniently and accessibly shelved during the year and their crowded condition relieved for a few years to come, although this arrangement is temporary and much more room will soon be required for the library.

A full list of accessions is herewith presented.

Respectfully submitted,

ARTHUR ROBINSON STONE,

E. I. M. Hall, *Librarian.*
Feb. 1, 1886.

1885.

AMERICAN.

Albany, N. Y. State Library. An. Report, 65–66, Cabinet Report 28, 33–37.

Baltimore, Md. Johns Hopkins University. Circulars, Vol. 4, Nos. 36–42. Vol. 5, Nos. 43–45, Biol. Lab. Studies, Vol. 3, Nos. 3–4.

Peabody Institute. 18 Annual Report, 1885.

Boston, Mass. Boston Soc. of Natural History. Proc. Vol. 22, Pts. 4–5. 23, Pts. 1–12, Mem. Vol. 3, Pt. 11.

Buffalo, N. Y. Young Men's Association. 49th Annual Report.

Cambridge, Mass. Museum of Comparative Zoology. Bulletin, Vol. 11, No. 11 ; 12, Nos. 1–2, Mem. Vol. 10, Nos. 2–4 ; 11, No. 1 ; 14, No. 1.

Peabody Museum Archaeology. Report, 1884–85.

Des Moines, Iowa. Des Moines Academy of Science. Bull. Vol. 1, No. 1.

Lawrence, Mass. Free Public Library. 13th Annual Report.

Lynn, Mass. Public Library. 22nd Annual Report.

Medford, Mass. Tufts College. Annual Report 1884–5, Cat., 1885.

Meriden, Conn. Scientific Association. Trans. Vol. 1, 1884.

Middletown, Conn. Wesleyan Univ. 12–13 Annual Report.

Minneapolis, Minn. Geol. and Nat. Hist. Survey. 1, 10, 11, 12. Annual Report, Survey Vol. 1, 1872–82.

Newton, Mass. Nat. Hist. Soc. Annual Report, 1883.

New York, New York. Amer. Mus. Nat. Hist. 16 Annual Report Bull. Vol. 1, No. 6.

Chamber of Commerce. Jour. Vol. 6, Nos. 4–5.

Metropolitan Museum of Art. 14th Annual Report, 1885-

N. Y. Microscopical Soc. Jour. Vol. 1, No. 1–7.

(24)

Philadelphia, Penn. Academy of Nat. Sciences. Proc., Nov.
–Dec., 1884 ; Jan.–July, 1885.
Amer. Entomological Soc. List of Coleoptera, Henshaw.
Amer. Naturalist. Vol. 19, Nos. 1–12.
Library Co. Bulletin, 1885.
Zoological Soc. 13th Annual Report, 1885.
Salem, Mass. Essex Institute. Bul. 15, Nos. 10–12 ; 16, Nos.
7–12 ; 17, Nos. 1–3.
San Francisco, Cal. Cal. Academy. Bulletin, Nos. 2–3.
Sedalia, Mo. Nat. Hist. Soc. Bulletin, No. 1.
St. Louis, Mo. Academy of Science. Transactions, Vol. 4,
No. 4, 1884.
Topeka, Kan. Kansas Academy of Sciences. Transactions,
Vol. 9, 16–17.
Washburn College. Bulletin, Vol. 1, No. 4.
Washington, D. C. Amer. Monthly Micros. Journal. Vol. 6,
Nos. 1–12.
Agriculture Dept. Report 1885, Cat. of Microscopes,
Grasses, and Report of Exhibition at New Orleans.
Astron. and Meteor. Observations. Vol. 28, 1881.
Dept. Interior. Circular of Information, Nos. 6–7, 1884,
1–2, 1885, 10th Census Report, Vol. 9, Hist. Sketches
of Universities and Colleges in U. S., Tertiary Verte-
brata.
Geological Survey. 3–4th Annual Reports, Bulletin, Nos.
2–14, Vols. 5–8, Surv., Geol. of Comstock Lode.
Fish Commission. Bulletin, Vol. 4, 1884.
Treasury Department. Finance Report, 1884.
U. S. Natural Museum. Proceedings, Vol. 7, Nos. 31–35,
8, 1–38, Bulletin, Vol. 1, No. 25.
Smithsonian Institution. Report, 1883. Contributions to
Knowledge, 24–25 ; Bureau of Ethnology, No. 3 ; List
of Foreign Correspondents, 1882–3.
War Department. Report of Expedition to Pt. Barrow,
Alaska.
Miscellaneous.
S. E. Cassino, Standard Natural History, Vols. 1, 2, 5.

Miscellaneous (Cont.).

E. S. Morse, 39 pamphlets, personal papers.

, Samuel Green, Library Aids.

Dr. Henry Wheatland, Historical Sketch of North Church, Salem.

F. W. Putnam, Remarks on chipped stone implements.

John Robinson, Forestry Bulletins, 1–5, 13.

S. M. Locke, American Apiculturist, Vols. 1–2.

J. Lawrence Smith, Original Researches in Mineralogy and Chemistry.

O. C. Marsh, Dinocerata, extinct order of gigantic mammal.

FOREIGN.

AUSTRIA.

Brunn. Naturforschenden Vereines. Verhandl. 1882.

Prague. K. K. Sternwarte. , Mag. und Met., 1884.

Wien. Kais. Akad. der Wissenschaften. Sitz.-ber. 1, 2, 6–10, 3, 4–10, 1883 ; 1, 2, 1–5, 3, 1–2, 1884 ; Denk. Bd., 47.

K. K. Geolog. Reichsanstalt. Jahrbuch, Bd. 35, Nos. 1–3, Verhandl. 13–18, 1884.

Verein zur Verbreitung natur. Kenntnisse. Schrifte 24, 1883–84.

BELGIUM.

Bruxelles. Academie Roy. des Sciences des Lettres et des Beaux Arts de Belgique. Annuaire Vol. 45, Bulletin, 3 Ser., Vol. 6–8, Mem. Cour. 45–46, autre Mem. 36, 3 pamphlets.

Soc. Entomologique de Belgique. Annales, 28–29.

Soc. Malacologique de Belgique. Annales 15, 18, 19, Proces-Verb., 1883–85.

Liège. Soc. Roy. des Sciences de Liège. Memoirs, Ser. 2, Tome 12.

BUENOS AIRES.

Buenos Aires. Officina Meteorologica Argentina. Annales, Tome 4.

DENMARK.

Copenhagen. L'Acad. Roy. de Copenhague. Bulletin, 2–3, 1884, 1, 1885, Memoirs, Vol. 1, Nos. 9–11, 2, 6–7.
Soc. Roy. des Antiquaires du Nord. Memoirs, 1885, Tillaeg., 1884, Aarboger, 3–4, 1884, 1–3, 1885.

FRANCE.

Cherbourg. Société Impériale des Sciences Naturelles. Memoirs 24, Cat. de la Bibliotheque, Pt. 2, 1883.
Lyon. Soc. Imp. des Sciences des Belles Lettres et des Arts. Memoirs, 27.
Soc. Linnéenne de Lyon. Annales, 30.
Paris. Soc. Entomologique de France. Bulletin, 18 Nos., March–Nov.
Soc. Géologique de France. Bulletin, Vol. 13, Nos. 1–7.

GERMANY.

Berlin. Entomologischer Verein. Zeit. Bd. 28, Heft 2, Inhalts Veizeichniss 29, 1.
Gesell. Naturforschender Freunde. Sitz. ber., 1884.
Konig Preus. Acad. der Wissen. Sitzungber. 1884, 1–39, 1885.
Bonn. Naturhistorischer Verein der preuss. Reinlande und Westfalen. Verhandl., 42, 1–2.
Braunschweig. Archiv. fur Anthropologie. Bd. 15 suppl. 16.
Bremen. Naturwissen. Vereine. Abhand., Bd. 9, Heft. 2.
Danzig. Naturforsch. Gesell. Schriften, Bd. 16, Heft 2.
Dresden. Naturwissenschaft. Gesell. Sitz. 1884, July–Dec., 1885, Jan.–June.
Emden. Naturforschenden Gesell. Jahr., 1883–84.
Erlangen. Physikalisch-Medicinische Gesell. Sitz. Bd. 16.
Hamburg. Verein fur Naturwissenschaftliche Unterhaltung. Verhandl., 1878–82.
Hanau. Naturhistorisk Tidskrift. Ser. 3, Vol. 14.
Konigsberg. Physikalisch-Okon. Gesell. Schriften, Bd. 25, 1–2, 1884–5.

Leipzig. Konig. sach. Gesell. der Wissenschaften. Berichte
1–2, 1883–84, 1–2, 1885.
Naturforsch. Gesell. Sitz., 1884.

Munchen. Kong. Bayr. Akad. der Wissen. Sitz. Math. Phys.
1–4, 1884, Phil. Hist. 1–6, 1884.

Munster. Westfal. Provinzial Vereines fur Wissen. und Kunst.
Jahr., 1884.

Wiesbaden. Nassauischen Verein fur Naturkunde. Jahrbucher, 37.

GREAT BRITAIN AND IRELAND.

Edinburg. Geological Soc. Trans., Vol. 4, Pt. 3 ; 5, Pt. 1.
Scottish Geographical Soc. Mag.Vol. 1, Nos. 1–12.

London. Entomological Soc. Trans., 1884.
Geological Soc., Q. F. 161–162, List of Soc., 1885.
Royal Geographical Soc., Proc. Vol. 6, 9–12 ; 7, 1–11.
Royal Soc. Phil. Trans., 175, 1–2, Proc. 37–33, 232–237.
The Council, 1884.
Zoological Soc., Proc., 1884, 3–4 ; 1885, 1–4.

Belfast. Naturalists' Field Club. Report, 1883–84.

Dublin. Royal Soc. Scien. Trans., Vol. 3, Pt. 4–6 ; Proc. Vol.
4, Pt. 5–6.

GREAT BRITAIN, COLONIES.

London, Ontario, Canada. Canadian Entomologist, Vol. 17,
1–11.

Montreal, Canada. Geological Survey of Canada. 1882–84.

Toronto, Ontario, Canada. Canadian Institute. Proc. Vol. 3,
Fasc. 1–2.
Entomological Soc. of Ont. Annual Report, 1884.

Winnipeg, Manitoba, Canada. Historical and Scientific Soc.
Report 1884, Trans. 12–18.

Halifax, Nova Scotia. N. S. Institute of Natural Science.
Proc. and Trans., Vol. 6, Pt. 2.

Calcutta, India. Geological Survey of India. Mem. P. I.,
Ser. 10, Vol. 3, Pt. 6, 13, Vol. 1, Pt. 4, Facs. 5, 14, Vol.
1, Pt. 5, Mem. Vol. 21, Pts. 1–4, Rec. Vol. 17, Pt. 4.
18, Pts. 1–3.

Sydney, New South Wales. Royal Soc. Jour. and. Proc., Vol. 18, 1884.

Adelaide, South Australia. Philosophical Soc. Vol. 7.

ITALY.

Firenze. Societa Entomologica. Bul. 1885, 1–4, Statute, 1885.

JAPAN.

Tokio. University of Tokio. Mem. No. 11.

MADAGASCAR.

Antananirivo. Antan. Annual and Madagas. Mag. Vols, 5–8, 1881–84.

MEXICO.

Mexico. El Museo Nacional. Anales Tom. 3, 3.

NETHERLANDS.

Amsterdam. Koniklijke Zoologisch Genootschap, " Natura Artis Magistra." Neder. Tidschrift voor de Dierkunde, Jaargang 5, no. 1.

Harlem. Teyler's Stichtning. Archiv, 1884.

NORWAY.

Trondhjem. Soc. Roy. des. Sciences. Skrifter, 1882.

RUSSIA.

Moscou. Soc. Imper. des Naturalistes de Moscou. Bulletin, 1–3, 1884, Nov. Mem. 14, 1883.

St. Petersbourg. Jardin Imper. de Botanique. Acta Horti Petro. Vol. 8, No. 3, 9, No. 1.

Soc. Entomologique de Russie. Horae ent. Soc. Ross. 7, 18.

SWEDEN.

Lund. Kongliga Universitetet. Acta Univ. 19, 1–4, 20, 1–4, Acc. Katalog, 1883–84.

Stockholm. Entomologist Tidskrift. Bd. 5, Heft 3–4, 1884.
Kong. Svenska Vetenskaps-Akad. Handl. 18–19, 1–2,
Oversigt, 38–40, Bihang 6, 7, 8, 1–2, Meteorolog. Jakt.
20–21, Lefnadsteckninger 2, Heft 2.
Sver. Geol. Undersokning. Aa, 88–96, Ab, 7–9, Bb, No.
3, C, 53–77, Ba, 4.

SWITZERLAND.

Basel. Naturforsch. Gesell. Verhandl. 7, Heft 3.
Geneve. L'Institut National Genevois. Bul. 26, Mem. 15,
1880–83.
Soc. de Physique et d'Histoire Naturelle. Mem. Vol. 28,
Pt. 2.
Lausanne. Soc. Vaudoise des Sciences Naturelles. Bul. 20,
No. 90–91.
Neuchatel. Soc. des Sciences Naturelles. Bul. 14, 1884.
St. Gallen. Naturwissenschaftlichen Gesell. Bericht, 1882–
83.